Promise Keeper

Parallels Between Moses and JESUS

Growing Faith Through God's Promises

by
Michael Beaumont

Reviewed by
Reverend Dr. Emmarex Okhakhu

CCB Publishing
British Columbia, Canada

Promise Keeper: Parallels Between Moses and JESUS

Copyright ©2017 by Michael Beaumont
ISBN-13   978-1-77143-335-8
First Edition

Library and Archives Canada Cataloguing in Publication
Beaumont, Michael, 1972-, author
Promise keeper : parallels between Moses and Jesus
/ by Michael Beaumont ; reviewed by Reverend Dr. Emmarex Okhakhu -- First edition.
Includes bibliographical references.
Issued in print and electronic formats.
ISBN 978-1-77143-335-8 (softcover).--ISBN 978-1-77143-336-5 (PDF)
1. Jesus Christ. 2. Moses (Biblical leader). 3. Bible. Gospels--Relation to the Old Testament.
4. Bible. Old Testament--Relation to the Gospels. I. Title.
BS2387.B44 2017   220.6   C2017-906027-9   C2017-906028-7

All Scriptural quotes are from the 1987 version of the KJV Bible and are in the Public Domain.
All images contained herein are in the Public Domain and are used without malice.
Cover artwork credit: Jesus walks on the water (Matthew 14) © ZU_09 | iStockphoto.com,
                     Crossing the Red Sea with Moses © Vlastas | Dreamstime.com
                     Three crosses image is in the Public Domain and is used without malice.

Fair Use Notice: This work contains minor excerpts of copyrighted material, the use of which has not always been specifically authorized by the copyright owner. It is believed this constitutes a 'fair use' of any such copyrighted material as provided for in section 107 of the US Copyright Law.

Reviewed by: Reverend Dr. Emmarex Okhakhu
Edited by: Susan Kohler

Disclaimer: This publication was designed to give the reader information on the subject matter covered. It is sold with the understanding that the authors are not engaged in giving legal, accounting or other advice outside the field of the authors' expertise. If other kinds of professional advice are needed, please seek competent professionals in those fields. It is not the purpose of this book to claim that this is the only book on the subject. The reader is urged to read all books on the subject and to learn as much as possible. Anyone who decides to follow the advice given in the book must do so with all due diligence. Every effort has been made to cover and research all aspects using the authors' own experiences. However, there may be mistakes, both typographical and in content. The purpose of this book is to educate and entertain. The authors and publisher shall have neither liability nor responsibility to any person or entity with respect to any loss or damage caused, or alleged to be caused, directly or indirectly by the information contained in this book. If you do not want to be bound by the above, you may return this book to the retailer for a full refund.

All rights reserved. No part of this publication may be reproduced, stored in a retrieval system or transmitted in any form or by any means, electronic, mechanical, photocopying, recording or otherwise without the express written permission of the publisher.

http://christianpartysupplies.org/promise-keeper-book
You can email the author at: uxodesign@gmail.com
Other books by Michael Beaumont:
• Duplicitous: How We the People Can Reclaim America
• Leading America: The Authentic Leader's Guide to Life, Liberty & the Pursuit of Happiness
• Dream 2 Achieve: Steps for Developing Today's Youth for Tomorrow's Leadership

Publisher: CCB Publishing
                 British Columbia, Canada
                 www.ccbpublishing.com

To God the Father, God the Son, and God the Holy Spirit
who inspired this book.

To those who are and/or want to know more
about being a follower of Christ.

Table of Contents

Prologue vii
Reviews ix
Introduction xiii

Chapter 1: Why This Book Is Important 1
    Perspectives on Christianity and the Bible 2
    Our Principles of Faith 8
    Our Approach to this Book 8

Chapter 2: Languages of the Bible 11
    Writing Systems and Culture 12
    Semitic Languages 14
    Hebrew Thought Patterns 14
    Conclusion 18

Chapter 3: Numbers in the Bible 20

Chapter 4: Seven Feasts 42
    Hebrew Calendar 42
    Passover / Pesach 45
    Feast of Unleavened Bread / Chag HaMatrzot 47
    Feast of Firstfruits / Reshit Katzir 49
    Feast of Weeks / Shavuot 50
    Feast of Trumpets / Rosh Hashanah 59
    Day of Atonement / Yom Kippur 62
    Feast of Tabernacles / Sukkot 63

Chapter 5: Bible as History 66
    Biblical Sequence of Events 70
    Biblical / Non-Biblical Links & Timeline 71
    Conclusion 115

Chapter 6: Trials and Tribulations 117
    Ten Plagues of Egypt 120
    Seal Trumpet Bowl Judgments 121
    Water Into Blood 123
    Frogs 124
    The Passover Lamb 126

Chapter 7: Servant Leadership 128
    Authentic Leadership 129
    7 Attributes of a Servant Leader 133
    Moses as a Servant Leader 137
    Time, Talents, and Treasure 139

Chapter 8: Parallels 144
    Feasts 144
    History 146
    Plagues 147
    Leadership 148
    Other 149

Chapter 9: Faith 156

Epilogue 163
About the Authors 165
Bibliography 168

Appendix 187
    Books of the Bible 187
    Apocrypha 188
    Kings of United Israel: 1052-931 BC 189
    Kings of Israel: 931-723 BC 189
    Kings of Judah: 931-587 BC 190
    Neo-Assyrian Empire Kings 192
    Neo-Babylonian Empire Kings 192

Prologue

by Sue Rebar

Promise Keeper is a book for every Christian seeking a greater revelation of God's plan through the performance of faith. Nothing is impossible with God.

Michael takes us on a journey of discovery providing historical and scientific facts along the way. Any believers desiring to grow their faith would be well served by reading and studying this book. Michael's research, education, and years of faithful study of God's Word archived in this book can catapult any believer's faith. He thoughtfully draws comparatives and applies history and science to confirm Biblical accounts.

I have known Michael for many years. We met on my own journey of faith. I am Co-Founder of two national public charities that provide services for military members, veterans, and their families. Welcome Home Troops has served tens of thousands since its inception in 2007. The Post 9-11 War Memorial Foundation is striving to restore the value of life by honoring the post September 11 casualties and their families. Along the journey I have had many revelations of applied Scripture, which became the model and structure of and for the creation of both charities.

Michael's discussion of the parallels between Moses and Jesus is just such an application of applied Scripture. As Christians we often don't understand why we feel a certain way or why we want to do something. Yet we choose to do things by faith. This book helps draw out your own faith in God and Scripture.

I have been so blessed to use applied Scripture for the concept of relationship building with Welcome Home Troops which resulted in a major study performed by Dr. Arthur Aron funded by a grant from the National Science Foundation. Our current project, the Post 9-11 War Memorial, is fully immersive and celebrates the lives of the fallen, and is inspired by Scripture.

Michael's intimate review of Biblical accounts of Jesus and Moses along with scientific and historical context will open your eyes to many things you may have never thought about before. By reading this book, you will be both challenged and edified to continue your journey as a person of strong Christian faith so that we can positively influence the lives of those around us, in this nation, and around the world.

Reviews

"Profound and powerful, this book can be the lever with which you can truly change your life."
- Carl B. Clark, Sr.

As I was putting the final touches on this book, I took an opportunity to lead a 6 week class on Bible History and Archaeology. It was hosted as a Sunday school class at Lawrence United Methodist Church near Indianapolis, Indiana. The main overarching concept of the class is that although the Holy Bible is not a history or science book, it is accurate in its description of various people, places, and events. As we gather more facts, we find that the Bible has been right all along. The concepts covered in the 6 classes are briefly described below:

Week 1: Thinking Like a Hebrew
- Fact, Opinion, and Truth
- Hebrew Calendar v. Roman Calendar
- 7 Feasts of Leviticus 23

Week 2: Life and Times of Jesus Christ
- 3 Historians Who Lived During the Julio-Claudian Dynasty
- Julio-Claudian Dynasty of Rome
- When Was Jesus Crucified?
- When Was Jesus Born?
- Alexander the Great, Hasmoneans, and Herodians

Week 3: Divided Kingdom
- Assyrian Kings in the Bible
- Babylonian Kings in the Bible
- Israel and Judah Kings in Assyrian and Babylonian Records
- 3 Temples of Israel

Week 4: Moses, Joshua, and Judges
- Egyptian Timeline
- Israel Timeline: Moses to Solomon
- Battle of Jericho
- Bronze Age Collapse
- Exodus and the Collapse of the Middle Kingdom of Egypt

Week 5: Genesis in 1 Session
- Mesopotamia Timeline
- Joseph and 12th Dynasty of Egypt
- Abraham and 3rd Dynasty of Ur
- War of Genesis 14
- Destruction of Sodom and Gomorrah
- Abraham – Moses Chronology
- Nimrod and the Tower of Babel
- Thoughts On Genesis 1-11

Week 6: Applying What We Have Learned
- Dead Sea Scrolls
- 70 Weeks of Daniel
- Jubilee

Reviews by those who attended the class:

"I enjoyed Mike's teaching. He is very knowledgeable and takes time to answer questions in class. I feel like I learned so much! Thank you for sharing your knowledge of the Bible." - Kim Morgan

"Fascinating material. Well researched and well taught. He knows this material and brings it to life. I want to learn so much more from this man's research. He is dedicated to the Bible's timeline and the proof of the truth of God's Word. Thank you from the bottom of my heart."
- Jane Ann Steiner

"This class was a wonderful experience in the teaching of the Bible in regards to events and timetables. The class brought events into context and showed proof of events from the Bible." - Judy Vigus

"Every Christian should experience this journey through history. It is very informative and helps the believer put history in context with dates and so many important events." - Elaine Bolton

"I enjoyed the class. You made each lesson informative and fun. You've presented yourself very well!" - Betty Harris

Introduction

"While strong winds uproot those with weak roots, those with resolute faith stand firm."
- Michael Beaumont

There is a story that has floated around for some time related to a pastor and a scientist. It has many variations, but it goes something like this. A pastor and a scientist begin their journey together to climb a mountain. The pastor packs light. He takes with him a Bible and an empty cup. Conversely, the scientist packs heavy. He takes a lot of clothes, food, water, research equipment, and scientific journals. After a short while, the scientist begins to breathe hard weighed down by so many things. The pastor, however, is whistling and full of energy. The scientist tires and they decide to split up. The two take different paths up the mountain top. The scientist takes wrong turns and gets lost a few times. Finally, he is so proud of himself that he made it to the top. He looks around and notices the pastor is already at the top. He is calm and rested. The pastor is drinking water from the cup he brought and is eating a sandwich. The pastor says graciously to the scientist, "glad to see that you made it up here," and offers him some food and water.

Did anybody make a wrong decision in this story? It might be easy to say that the scientist was incorrect because he packed heavy and made many wrong turns. In this scenario, it was the pastor who was wrong. He did not take the time to help guide the scientist. Part of a pastor's burden is to teach and guide those who do not know the way. The pastor could have stayed with the scientist, helped carry the load, and guided them toward the correct path. Another option is to go through all the baggage together before the journey began to see what could be left behind. Then the scientist would not have tired so easily.

Similarly, this book acts as a guide for those who do not know. It is not the Bible, which is the ultimate source of truth, and it does not pretend to be. This book provides thoughts, ideas, information, and inspiration about the lives of Moses and Jesus. We take you on a journey of discovery that looks at Moses and Jesus through many facets, to develop a more complete picture of who they are and what they represent. We look at events and people surrounding their lives. We discuss some of their teachings and their behaviors, and examine some of the languages they spoke.

Our purpose as authors of this book is not to convince you beyond a shadow of a doubt that people and events described within the Bible are historical facts or that we have all the answers. There has been, and always will be, a strong element of faith needed when it comes to a personal relationship with Jesus Christ. Hebrews 11:6 states, "Without faith it is impossible to please him: for he that comes to God must believe that He is, and that He is a rewarder of them that diligently seek Him [KJV]."

We want to provide you with knowledge and ideas that introduce you to and strengthen your faith in Jesus Christ, the author of our salvation. We want to help you understand more fully why you believe and offer you opportunities for your faith to grow deeper. We do this by studying the lives of Moses and Jesus, and discovering literal and symbolic connections between these two men of the Bible. Through the narratives provided, some of God's grand design, purpose, and power are revealed. Pieces of the puzzle are placed into a framework of increased understanding.

When did Jesus and Moses live? Why do four books of the Old Testament spend so much time describing Moses and his life? Why do four books of the New Testament spend so much time describing Jesus and his life? Why should we as believers want to learn more about the promises described in the Bible, some of which were written by Moses, and how Jesus is the fulfillment of those promises? We demonstrate that many things in the Bible, as seen through the lives of Jesus and Moses, are not random – that they do follow a master plan – and that these events occur according to God's perfect will.

Moses and Jesus were born over 1500 years apart. Moses was born of a servant and raised as a prince of Egypt. Jesus is a prince who became a servant in land controlled by the Roman Empire. With such opposites, and that they lived thousands of years ago, how are they relevant to us in the 21st Century and beyond?

For those who follow Christ, and want to be more like Him, we have this hunger and thirst to learn more, to do more, and to become more, so that we can be an effective beacon of truth to the world. We as authors want to inform you of some of the things we have learned to help guide and inspire you. What we write is not truth, but just our limited understanding of it from the perspective of flawed human beings. We want to reveal to you what has been revealed to us through careful study and fervent prayer regarding two incredible servant leaders. It is our hope that through reading this book, you have not only learned a little, but that you have become inspired to become more like Him who was there at the beginning of time.

Enjoy!

Chapter 1

Why This Book Is Important

*"There are two great days in a person's life -
the day we are born and the day we discover why."*
- William Barclay

It was the summer of 2016. Jen (my significant other) and I were attending a church service in Indianapolis. The pastor said one sentence in passing about the similarities between Jesus and Moses. Little did he or we know what was to follow. We were curious and began our own internal discussion and research. We noticed two things. First, there are numerous similarities. Second, there is limited information out there related to this overarching concept. We both started reading the Torah (Genesis, Exodus, Leviticus, Numbers, Deuteronomy) and the Gospels (Matthew, Mark, Luke, John) in much more detail. We immediately started to notice dozens of similarities. There is no way this was random.

As a result of this research, we developed a children's Bible party theme called "Promise Keepers" that introduced some of these similarities between Jesus and Moses. We developed and presented some of these similarities in public forums, Sunday school classes, and meetings. There was such a demand for this information that we decided to publish a book – this book – to discuss these ideas in more systematic detail.

Being a Christian and being in fellowship with Christ Jesus is so much more than just accepting Him as our Savior and Redeemer and calling it a day. It is the daily practice of open and honest communication. It is the daily toil of study and research. It is the daily journey of discovery as to how we can help make positive and permanent changes in the lives of others.

Being a Christian is not about short-lived happiness that is founded on our own pleasure. Truly being a follower of Christ is to be filled with sacrificial love, overwhelming joy, a peace that passes all understanding, and unyielding faithfulness. We cannot accomplish these things by our own strength, but through the power and wisdom of having a regular and personal relationship with our Creator and our Guide. As it says in Romans 8:31, "If God be for us, who can be against us [KJV]?"

We would like to spend the remainder of this chapter discussing our perspectives on Christianity and the Bible, our principles of faith, and our approach to writing this book.

Perspectives on Christianity and the Bible

The Holy Bible is the most read book in the history of the world. Guinness Book of World Records lists it as the Best-Selling Book of all time. It is the most translated and distributed book by far. Approximately 5 billion copies have been printed and distributed in over 1300 translations. Also, there are about 2.2 billion Christians in the world, which represents about one-third of the world's population. Let's take this a step further. Christianity, Judaism, and Islam link themselves to Abraham, Noah, and Adam. This accounts for almost 4 billion people or about 54% of the world's population. Even Hinduism and Buddhism, which account for over 19% of the world's population, relate stories of a Great Flood. As a comparison, less than 15% of the world's population do not believe in some higher power. It is no small thing that religions that directly affect almost three-quarters of the world's population have overlap related to the origins of man and a Great Flood. So how did this happen?

To be a Christian is to be a follower of Christ. His life and teachings are described in the Bible, specifically the Gospels (Matthew, Mark, Luke, John). Many might get turned off by how big the Bible is with its 66 books, 1189 chapters, and 31,102 verses. I have heard many reasons. It's too big. It's complicated. It was written a long time ago by people who do not understand my problems. It contradicts science. It contradicts itself.

For as big as the Bible is, there is a simple, consistent, and coherent message. If you know and understand five verses, you understand the true purpose of the Bible and what it truly means to be a follower of Christ:

Matthew 22:37-39 - "...You shall love the Lord your God with all your heart, and with all your soul, and with all your mind. This is the first and great commandment. And the second is like unto it: You shall love your neighbor as yourself [KJV]."

John 3:16 - "For God so loved the world, that He gave His only begotten Son, that whosoever believes in Him should not perish, but have everlasting life [KJV]."

John 14:6 - "...I am the way, the truth, and the life: no man comes unto the Father, but by Me [KJV]."

The message is simple and consistent throughout the Bible. God loves you. Believe in Christ's sacrifice for you. Love God. Love others. Christianity is not a checklist of things you can and cannot do. Christianity is about the faith, hope, and love in our lives that come from knowing Jesus. The more you understand these things, the more you want to know. This is the primary reason we wrote this book.

This book is for those who want to swim in deeper waters. It is for those who want to know a lot more about the content of the Bible. It connects some of the ideas in the Old Testament as seen through the life of Moses with ideas in the New Testament as seen through the life of Jesus. It places concepts and ideas as related through stories and narratives into a "Big Picture," which is that Jesus is our Promise Keeper.

There are numerous variations of communities that are lumped together as "Christian." Some of these denominations include: Adventist, Anglican, Apostolic, Baptist, Catholic, Church of Christ, Eastern Orthodox, Evangelical, Latter Day Saint, Lutheran, Messianic Jew, Methodist, Pentecostal, Presbyterian, Unitarian, and more. The issue is that these disparate groups do not necessarily believe in the same things or even use the same "Bible." For example, the Catholic Church recognizes 73 books of the Bible, whereas many Protestant denominations recognize 66 books. So who is right, and how can I trust either one since they cannot even agree on the same source of information?

Let's provide a little historical perspective on the reason for some different versions of the Bible. The Hebrew Bible, also known as the Masoretic text, contains 24 books. These books were primarily written in Hebrew between the 15th and 4th Centuries BC. Hebrew scribes have been responsible for passing these texts from one generation to the next. The Old Testament of the Protestant Bible contains the same information as the Masoretic text. It is just reorganized and translated into 39 books (see Appendix).

The Septuagint was the version of the Bible used by Hellenistic Jews. The Septuagint represents a Greek translation of the Bible by 70 Jewish scholars. The Bible the Catholic and Eastern Orthodox churches use are based on this Greek translation of the Old Testament, which contains additional books in the Old Testament known as the Apocrypha (see Appendix). Some of these Apocryphal books were written as recently as the 2nd Century BC. Where the Masoretic text was preserved by Jewish scholars, the Septuagint was preserved by church scholars. Both the Catholic and Protestant Bibles contain identical information in the New Testament.

So which version of the Holy Bible is correct? The answer can be found within the concept of canonicity. To be part of the Holy Bible canon is to be part of a collection or list of sacred books regarded as inspired by God and widely accepted as genuine. The development of the Holy Bible canon was not an individual event. It came to be through centuries of study and use by believers, scholars, pastors, priests, and institutions.

It was Athanasius, the 20th bishop of Alexandria (328–373 AD), who provided the first complete list of the Holy Bible canon. He was a Christian theologian primarily a member of the Coptic Orthodox Church. He spent over 17 years in exile ordered by four different Roman emperors (Constantine I, Constantius II, Julian, and Valens).

In 325 AD, Athanasius was a deacon and assistant to Bishop Alexander of Alexandria during the First Council of Nicaea. Roman emperor Constantine I convened this council in May–August 325 AD. It was composed of theologians and Biblical scholars. It was the first effort to attain wide consensus within the Church of some Christian principles. The list of the 66 books of the Bible were the only books universally accepted as inspired by God.

In the first and second centuries AD, many writings were circulating among the Christians. Gradually the need to have a definite list of the inspired Scriptures became apparent. Heretical movements were rising, each one choosing its own selected Scriptures, including such documents as the Gospel of Thomas, the Shepherd of Hermas, the Apocalypse of Peter, and the Epistle of Barnabas. Gradually it became widely accepted which works were truly genuine and which mixed truth with fantasy. By the end of the fourth century the canon of 66 books was definitively settled and accepted.

The Apocrypha represents books of the Holy Bible which are accepted by some Christian denominations, but are not universally accepted. They contain interesting incites and stories, but are not universally accepted as inspired by God. The Apocrypha includes: 1 Esdras, 2 Esdras, 1 Macabees, 2 Macabees, Judith, and Tobias.

Most of us cannot read Hebrew, Aramaic, or Greek. Also, we do not have original copies of the books of the Bible. Therefore, we must find a reasonable alternative, which is to find an English translation of the Bible that stays as true as possible to the original inspired Word of God.

There are three basic philosophies employed in the translation of the

Bible into English. The first is word for word. Some of these translations include: Amplified (AMP), English Standard Version (ESV), King James Version (KJV), New American Bible (NAB), New American Standard Bible (NASB), and New King James Version (NKJV). The second is thought for thought. Some of these translations include: Contemporary English Version (CEV) and International Children's Bible (ICB). The third is a balance between word for word and thought for thought. Some of these translations include: God's Word Translation (GWT), Holman Christian Standard Bible (HCSB), New Century Version (NCV), New International Version (NIV), and New Living Translation (NLT).

It is the King James Version of the Bible that we primarily use for studies and quotes in this book. The King James Version of the Bible was completed in 1611 AD. King James insisted on the most accurate translation possible to be performed by the best scholars in England.

Some of the Bible quotes used in this book have been modified slightly. We have replaced words like "Thee" and "Thou" with "You" and "Your." We have also replaced words like "Believeth" with "Believes." Our goal was to keep to original content as much as possible while making them a little easier to read.

Each Bible translation has its own system to translate the Bible from Hebrew, Aramaic, and Greek into English. We recommend that you familiarize yourself with multiple versions of the Bible to identify the similarities and differences.

Our Principles of Faith

<u>Inspiration and inerrancy of the Bible</u>: The Bible, in its original form, is the inspired word of God and truth. God, the Creator and Ruler of this world and universe, has given us His Word, the Bible. The Bible is to serve as a guide for our lives.

<u>Virgin birth and deity of Christ</u>: Jesus is both God and Man. He was born of a virgin, and is the Son of God. Both Mary and Joseph are of the bloodline of King David.

<u>Trinity of God</u>: God the Father, God the Son, and God the Holy Spirit are three separate aspects of a single God.

<u>Substitutionary atonement of Christ</u>: Jesus was executed via crucifixion. He was the perfect sacrificial lamb, who took on our sins and imperfections: past, present, and future.

<u>Resurrection of Christ from the dead</u>: The death of Jesus would be meaningless without His subsequent resurrection. Not only would He not be that much different from other men, He would also not have as much authority to grant us freedom from eternal death. Everyone still must face the death of the body, but Christians do not need to fear the death of the spirit.

<u>Return of Christ</u>: Jesus promised His disciples that He will return. He is to return as King.

Our Approach to this Book

This book uses both a factual and theological approach to

understanding concepts within the Bible. Science and Christianity are not in conflict with each other. They complement each other. The primary reason why these supposed conflicts exist is because of our egos and our conclusions based on limited knowledge and understanding. We often fill in the gaps of understanding with incorrect assumptions based on our personal experiences and desires. The more we learn and understand, the more we realize that the Bible has been correct all along.

It is not within the scope of this book to prove or disprove the existence of anything. We are simply revealing truth as it has been revealed to us. Through diligent study and prayer, we have learned a great deal about the interconnectedness of the lives of Moses and Jesus. We look for those places where facts gathered from science and information gathered from the Bible are in harmony with each other. We provide context and a framework for those facts and ideas to develop a "Big Picture" narrative and a deeper understanding of both Moses and Jesus. The focus of this book is more about the story than about the details. Enough facts and details are offered to substantiate certain conclusions while attempting to avoid so much detail that we lose sight of our main objectives.

We use the term "truth," but what exactly does that mean? Truth is more related to fact than opinion. A fact is something we can observe or measure. It is based on something we can hear, see, smell, taste, or touch. An opinion is our own subjective ideas and perceptions. It is our own personal thoughts about how the world exists, is organized, and functions. Truth is God's objective reality. It is how the pieces of the puzzle fit together within God's perfect purpose and will. It is the big picture or tapestry in which facts are pieced or woven together. It is the construct that forms the foundation of our thoughts and actions. Truth is not about consensus, arbitrary perceptions, or our own personal concepts. Truth is how God sees us and the universe around us.

The first five words of the Bible are: "In the beginning God created." Deuteronomy 32:4 says, "He is the Rock, His work is perfect: for all His ways are judgment: a God of truth and without iniquity, just and right is He [KJV]." God is our Creator. He alone is the standard bearer of truth, and the Bible is His personal message to us.

This book is not about us, our research, our conclusions, or our egos. This book is about you and your desire to want to learn more, do more, and be more as related to Jesus our Messiah. It is less about how we write the content, and more about how you receive this content. As described in Luke 8:4-8, let these words fall on good soil. Let them enrich you so that you can learn, grow, and bear fruit.

Some information we provide may be inaccurate, and some of our conclusions may be wrong. We do not promise perfection, but we do promise that we have done our research and have provided substantiated facts and compelling evidence to support our conclusions. We also promise that, to the best of our ability, we will clearly separate objective facts from subjective opinions. At the end of the day, it is our goal for you to have a greater understanding about the lives of both Moses and Jesus, and that it helps grow your faith in Jesus Christ as Promise Keeper, Redeemer, Savior, and Lord.

Chapter 2

Languages of the Bible

*"Kindness is the language which
the deaf can hear and the blind can see."*
- Mark Twain

The Holy Bible was written primarily in Hebrew, Aramaic, and Greek, but the common languages of our modern societies are English, French, Mandarin, and Spanish. Language does play a role in both how we transmit information and how we receive information.

What is language, and what is it used for? Human language is acquired from and used for social interactions. Human interactions and social culture are complex and require tools to accommodate for this. Language is one tool that is used extensively. More specifically, language is the use of complex abstract systems to communicate. The scientific study of language is called linguistics.

Natural languages, such as English, Hebrew, and Greek, are typically spoken. However, any system can be encoded using auditory, visual, or tactile stimuli to create language, such as whistling, Morse Code, or braille. The most fundamental aspect of language is that it is a set of rules used to communicate thoughts, ideas, and meanings. The use of language is deeply entrenched in and inseparable from culture. Languages express meaning by relating concrete objects to abstract meaning. For example, a neon sign contains the letters O P E N. The concrete object is the four letters in a specific sequence.

The abstract cultural meaning is that you are invited to walk in, look around, ask questions, and purchase something that you might need or want.

Writing Systems and Culture

The use of writing has made language more useful to humans. It makes it possible to store large amounts of information outside the human body and retrieve it again. It allows for communication across time and space. We can read Homer's epic adventure, the Iliad, written in the 8th Century BC, Chinese General Sun Tzu's Art of War written in the 5th Century BC, or Meditations by Roman Emperor Marcus Aurelius written in the 2nd Century AD. We can also read about how the Israelites left Egypt to establish their own nation, which was written by Moses in the 15th Century BC (see Chapter 5).

The invention of the first writing systems is roughly contemporary with the beginning of the Bronze Age in the late 4th millennium BC (~3200 BC). Sumerian archaic cuneiform script and Egyptian hieroglyphs are generally considered to be the earliest writing systems. When modern Egyptologists started finding ancient artifacts with hieroglyphs in the late 1700s, they were unsure as to their meaning, or how the language sounded. The people who made them had been gone for thousands of years, and the culture that produced them no longer existed. So how are we able to understand ancient documents such as these?

In the case of Egyptian hieroglyphs, we had the Rosetta Stone. This stone was discovered during a Napoleonic expedition of the Nile delta in 1799. It was created in 196 BC and contained a decree by

Ptolemy V Epiphanes written in three languages: ancient Egyptian hieroglyphs, Demotic Egyptian script, and ancient Greek. Even with this stone, it took academics another 30 years to effectively translate Egyptian hieroglyphs. A French man by the name of Jean-François Champollion was the person who finally cracked the code. He compared the modern Coptic language (a spoken Egyptian language) with written Demotic script and found numerous similarities. He then continued working backwards using Coptic and Demotic to translate the hieroglyphs. Through this process, we are now able to better understand the culture that produced Egyptian hieroglyphs.

Also, certain similar attributes within writing systems can be used to find similarities, and even lineages, between languages. As an example, let's look at writing direction. The direction used in a writing system is entirely arbitrary and established by cultural rules. Latin and Germanic based languages, such as Italian, Spanish, French, Dutch, and English are read from left to right. Many Latin and Germanic groups interacted significantly with each other during the rise and fall of the Roman Empire.

Hebrew, Arabic, Aramaic, Coptic, and early Greek are read from right to left. Because of this writing direction, and because of close geographic proximity with each other, these languages are probably derived from or influenced by a common language, such as Phoenician. The Phoenicians were a great sea-faring nation based near modern day Lebanon that owed much of its wealth to trade throughout the Mediterranean region and Fertile Crescent. They became established around 1500 BC and developed the first known consonant based alphabet system that potentially influenced most other alphabet based writing systems known today. We will also learn later in this book (Chapter 5) that there may have been another source of written language within the land of the Tigris and Euphrates Rivers, also known as Mesopotamia.

Semitic Languages

Semitic languages are a group of similar Afroasiatic languages originating in the Middle East. These extant and extinct languages include: Akkadian, Amharic, Ammonite, Amorite, Arabic, Aramaic, Assyrian, Babylonian, Eblaite, Edomite, Ge'ez, Hebrew, Maltese, Mariotic, Moabite, Phoenician, Punic, Syriac, Tigrinya, and Ugaritic. These languages have been grouped together based on similarities in vocabulary, grammar, structure, and morphology. Essentially, this means that these languages are closely related to each other and probably have all been derived from a common ancestor. Semitic languages are currently spoken by more than 330 million people throughout Western Asia, North Africa, North America, and Europe. The term "Semitic" was first used in the 1780s by members of the Göttingen School of History who derived the name from Shem, one of the three sons of Noah in the Book of Genesis. According to Genesis 11, Abraham is a descendant of Noah through Shem.

Hebrew Thought Patterns

Hebrew is the language of the Old Testament, which was partially written by Moses – who was educated as an Egyptian prince. It would not be difficult to imagine that because of his heritage and upbringing he would be literate in multiple languages, especially Egyptian and Hebrew. Since culture and language are inseparable, as described above, knowing cultural context of the Bible would help us better understand its meanings. Mark 10:25 states, "It is easier for a camel to go through the eye of a needle, than for a rich man to enter into the kingdom of God [KJV]." This verse is not describing needle and thread, which would be a common misconception in modern American culture. The "Eye of the Needle" is a gate, which opened after the main gate was closed at night. A camel could only pass through this smaller gate if it was stooped and had its baggage removed. It was designed for security reasons so that enemies could not simply ride into the city on their camels and attack.

The Old Testament was written almost exclusively in Hebrew. Therefore, it is tied to Hebrew culture, thoughts, and meanings. As with much of Hebrew writings, there are four ways to interpret the Bible. The first is a simple, literal, and straightforward approach. What you see is what you get. The second is the implied meaning. The scriptures let you figure it out for yourself, but it provides some clues or hints. The third is the moral meaning of the passage. What is the Bible saying about how we should live our lives? The fourth is about interpretation and hidden meanings. For example, Genesis 5 describes the genealogy from Adam to Noah. It is straightforward, or is it? Names of the characters in the Bible relate their own meanings. If we look at the names within the genealogy of Noah in order, we find several layers of truth within the same message:

Adam (man)
Seth (appointed)
Enosh (mortal)
Kenan (sorrow);
Mahalalel (blessed God)
Jared (shall come down)
Enoch, (teaching)

Methuselah (his death shall bring)
Lamech (the despairing)
Noah (comfort).

First, we read the literal genealogy from Adam to Noah. Second, we have an opportunity to learn from the lives of these people as described in Genesis, such as Adam (Genesis 2-5) and Noah (Genesis 5-9). Third, we observe how God is consistent in both righteousness and grace in how He interacts with mankind. Fourth, we find a hidden message written in the genealogy itself. If we translate the meanings of the names in the genealogy, we get the following message:

Man appointed mortal sorrow, blessed God shall come down teaching. His death shall bring the despairing comfort.

This is profound. It demonstrates that even in the earliest chapters of the Book of Genesis (which was written almost 3500 years ago), God had already laid out His plan of redemption for mankind. The Bible is an integrated message system and a product of supernatural engineering. Every number, every place name, and every detail is there for our learning, our discovery, and our amazement.

Just as Hebrew gives us four levels of understanding, the four Gospels of the New Testament give us four accounts from four perspectives and four personalities. Each Gospel was written for a distinct purpose. Each author wanted the reader to know the truth about Jesus from a specific perspective. To accomplish this purpose, each Gospel is aimed at a certain audience and each writer is selective of the people and events he includes. They can be summed up in the following way:

Matthew: Jesus is the Son of David
Mark: Jesus is the Son of Man
Luke: Jesus is the Son of Adam
John: Jesus is the Son of God

The four Gospels were written to describe four aspects of the life and ministry of Jesus Christ. Each gospel writer wrote from a different perspective to a different audience. In Matthew, Jesus is the king. In Mark, Jesus is the servant. In Luke, Jesus is the perfect man. In John, Jesus is God. When the Gospels are compared with each other, we get a complete portrait of Jesus. He was God from all eternity who came down to earth as the perfect man. He was the Messiah of Israel, the King of the Jews, the one who did the job that God sent Him to do.

Greek Thought Patterns

Where Hebrew is about layers and texture, Greek is about precision. Greek thought is something that is nailed down. Each word means exactly and only one thing. Fourteen of the twenty-seven books in the New Testament have traditionally been attributed to Paul. He was a Pharisee and a Roman citizen. He was probably well-educated. He more than likely spoke and wrote in the common and influential languages of that region: Hebrew, Latin, and Greek. Something to keep in mind is that the authors of the New Testament were from a mixture of cultures, languages, and backgrounds. One would expect to find a mixed bag of styles, and indeed we do (as described above with the four Gospels). The Greek language is precise and deliberate as demonstrated in the New Testament which uses four separate words for "love." Each variation has a specific meaning.

Phileo is used in John 21:15-17 and describes companionship and friendship.
Agape is used in John 3:16 and describes a pure Godly love. It is a love of esteem, evaluation, and self-sacrifice.
Storge is used in Romans 1:31 and describes a natural affection or obligation, such as that between a parent and child.
Eros is described in Song of Solomon. The entire book is about a deep passionate love (both emotional and physical).

Conclusion

Language reflects the culture it belongs to. Hebrew is textured and layered. The Old Testament, written partially by Moses, is textured and layered. Greek is precise. The New Testament is specific in how it describes people and events.

Saint Augustine (354–430 AD) was an early Christian theologian and philosopher who lived in the region now known as Algeria in North Africa. He said this about the Bible, "The new is in the old concealed; the old is in the new revealed." The Bible, with all its details, texture, and nuance, has a singular purpose. John 3:16 states that purpose this way: "For God so loved the world, that He gave His only begotten Son, that whosoever believes in Him should not perish, but have everlasting life [KJV]."

The two testaments of the Bible are closely interrelated with each other. The key to understanding the New Testament is to see in it the fulfillment of promises revealed in the Old Testament. The Old Testament points forward in time, preparing God's people for the work of Christ in the New Testament. Genesis, the first book of the Bible and the first book attributed to Moses, starts with the beginning of the universe and the creation of man. This was shortly followed by man's destruction through the sins of Adam and Eve. The remainder of the Bible, from Genesis chapter 3 to Revelation chapter 22, is about God's work of redeeming a fallen humanity.

The Book of Genesis gives us an overview of the patriarchal period and the covenants that God made with them. They form the foundation for everything that follows in redemptive history. Genesis ends with the children of Israel migrating into Egypt to be rescued by the intervention of Joseph, who ruled as the nation's vizier or prime minister. Exodus opens with the Israelites having been governed with benevolence under Joseph who are now in bondage under Pharaoh. The Book of Exodus is a narrative of divine intervention to free the Israelites from the strongest military force in the world. Leviticus is about the laws governing worship, ritual, and the establishment of the priesthood, all of which foreshadow the work of Jesus Christ. Leviticus 23 sums up the work of Jesus Christ as described through the establishment of seven feasts: Passover, Unleavened Bread, First fruits, Pentecost, Trumpets, Atonement, and Tabernacles (see Chapter 4). Numbers and Deuteronomy continue to develop the historical patterns of the experiences of Israel from the days of the Exodus to the passing of Moses. Genesis through Deuteronomy set up the framework for our comprehensive understanding of what it means to be a follower of Christ as related to both hardship and fulfilled promises as demonstrated in the four Gospels.

Chapter 3

Numbers in the Bible

*"God blessed the seventh day, and sanctified it:
because that in it He had rested from all
His work which God created and made."*
- Genesis 2:3 [KJV]

Just as text has meaning in the Bible, so too do numbers. The study of numbers in the Bible is called biblical numerology. It is the idea that the use of a specific number, such as the number 7, has both a literal and symbolic meaning within the Bible. A week as used in the Bible refers to 7 days or years. Its symbolic meaning is that of spiritual completeness or perfection. Whether numbers have significance in the Bible is not accepted by all Biblical scholars. We believe the Bible uses numbers to develop patterns or to teach spiritual truth.

Not every number in the Bible has symbolic meaning. Sometimes it is just a number. Chapter and verse numbers have no validity or significance because those were added much later by men to make it easier to organize and add structure to the Bible. Initially, books of the Bible were only separated into paragraphs and sections. Septuagint scholars rearranged the books of the Bible based on chronology and sequence of events.

Archbishop Stephen Langton was an English Cardinal of the Roman Catholic Church and Archbishop of Canterbury between 1207 AD until his death in 1228 AD. The dispute between King John of England and Pope Innocent III over his election was a major factor in the production of the Magna Carta in 1215 AD. It is the chapter and verse system developed by Stephen Langton that is used today. Understanding the symbolism of numbers in the Bible can help us to decipher patterns within the Bible. It can lead us to a deeper understanding of spiritual truth within the Bible.

1 = Union, Unity

- Genesis 2:24 - "Therefore shall a man leave his father and his mother, and shall cleave unto his wife: and they shall be one flesh [KJV]."
- Genesis 11:1 - "The whole earth was of one language, and of one speech [KJV]."
- Exodus 26:11 - "You shall make fifty taches (hooks or clasps) of brass, and put the taches into the loops, and couple the tent together, that it may be one [KJV]."
- Deuteronomy 6:4 - "Hear, O Israel: The Lord our God is one Lord [KJV]."
- Ephesians 4:5 - "One Lord, one faith, one baptism [KJV]."

One is used 2444 times in the New King James Version of the Bible. Most of the time, it is used to notate a number, a single person or a single item. Once in a great while, as seen in the examples above, it is used to symbolize a union or unity.

Psalm 133:1 states, "Behold, how good and how pleasant it is for brethren to dwell together in unity [KJV]!" Ephesians 4:1-6 states, "I therefore, the prisoner of the Lord, beseech you that you walk worthy of the vocation wherewith you are called, with all lowliness and meekness, with longsuffering, forbearing one another in love; endeavouring to keep the unity of the Spirit in the bond of peace. There is one body, and one Spirit, even as you are called in one hope of your calling; one Lord, one faith, one baptism, one God and Father of all, who is above all, and through all, and in you all [KJV]." We are called as Christians to be united in faith, hope, and love. We are to love as Christ loved. We are to demonstrate compassion and charity toward others. This is not done through our own power, but through the power of the Holy Spirit.

2 = Companionship, Division, Witnessing

- Genesis 1:16 - "God made two great lights; the greater light to rule the day, and the lesser light to rule the night: He made the stars also [KJV]."
- Genesis 6:19 - "And of every living thing of all flesh, two of every sort shall you bring into the ark, to keep them alive with you; they shall be male and female [KJV]."
- Genesis 25:23 - "The Lord said unto her, 'Two nations are in your womb, and two manner of people shall be separated from your bowels; and the one people shall be stronger than the other people; and the elder shall serve the younger' [KJV]."
- Joshua 2:1 - "Joshua the son of Nun sent out of Shittim two men to spy secretly, saying, 'Go view the land, even Jericho.' And they went, and came into a harlot's house, named Rahab, and lodged there [KJV]."
- Judges 15:13 - "They spoke unto him, saying, 'No, but we will bind you fast, and deliver you into their hand; but surely we will not kill you.' And they bound him with two new cords, and brought him up from the rock [KJV]."

- 1 Samuel 6:7 - "Now therefore make a new cart, and take two milch kine (milk cows), on which there have come no yoke, and tie the kine (cows) to the cart, and bring their calves home from them [KJV]."
- Mark 6:7 - "And He called unto Him the twelve, and began to send them forth by two and two; and gave them power over unclean spirits [KJV]."
- Revelation 11:3 - "I will give power unto my two witnesses, and they shall prophesy a thousand two hundred and threescore (sixty) days, clothed in sackcloth [KJV]."
- Revelation 11:4 - "These are the two olive trees, and the two candlesticks standing before the God of the earth [KJV]."
- Revelation 13:11 - "I beheld another beast coming up out of the earth, and he had two horns like a lamb and spoke as a dragon [KJV]."

Two is used 740 times in the New King James Version of the Bible. Most of the time, it is used to notate a number or a couple items. Once in a great while, as seen in the examples above, it is used symbolically for several purposes. In the case of Mark 6:7 and other similar verses, it denotes evangelism and witnessing. In the case of Genesis 6:19, it is related to companionship. In the case of Genesis 1:16, it is related to division or separation.

1 Peter 3:8 calls us as believers to be of one mind having compassion and love for one another. 1 Peter 3:15 calls us to always be ready to explain the hope that is within us. Matthew 28:19-20 calls us to teach others and baptize them in the name of God the Father, Son, and Holy Ghost. The Holy Spirit comes along side us to teach us, guide us, and encourage us. We are called to do the same to others through the authority and power of God.

3 = Divine Completeness, Divine Perfection, Trinity

- Genesis 40:10,12 - "In the vine were three branches: and it was as though it budded, and her blossoms shot forth; and the clusters thereof brought forth ripe grapes. And Joseph said to him, 'This is the interpretation of it: The three branches are three days.' [KJV]."
- Deuteronomy 16:16 - "Three times in a year shall all your males appear before the Lord your God in the place which He shall choose; in the Feast of Unleavened Bread, and in the Feast of Weeks, and in the Feast of Tabernacles: and they shall not appear before the Lord empty [KJV]."
- 1 Samuel 30:12 - "They gave him a piece of a cake of figs, and two clusters of raisins: and when he had eaten, his spirit came again to him: for he had eaten no bread, nor drunk any water, three days and three nights [KJV]."
- Esther 4:16 - "Go, gather together all the Jews that are present in Shushan, and fast for me, and neither eat nor drink three days, night or day: I also and my maidens will fast likewise; and so will I go in unto the king, which is not according to the law: and if I perish, I perish [KJV]."
- Daniel 7:5 - "Behold another beast, a second, like a bear, and it raised up itself on one side, and it had three ribs in the mouth of it between the teeth of it: and they said thus unto it, 'Arise, devour much flesh' [KJV]."
- Jonah 1:17 - "Now the Lord had prepared a great fish to swallow up Jonah. And Jonah was in the belly of the fish three days and three nights [KJV]."
- Matthew 26:61 - "This fellow said, 'I am able to destroy the temple of God, and to build it in three days' [KJV]."

- Matthew 27:63 - "Saying, 'Sir, we remember that that deceiver said, while he was yet alive, after three days I will rise again' [KJV]."

Three is used 440 times in the New King James Version of the Bible. In the case of Deuteronomy 16:16, it refers to the Trinity. God the Father, God the Son, and God the Holy Spirit are three aspects of the same God. The Feast of Unleavened Bread references the work of Jesus as the sacrificial lamb being the substitute for our sins. The Feast of Weeks – and Jubilee which is a week of weeks - reference the work of the Holy Spirit. The Feast of Tabernacles references God the Father's work. These feasts are described in more detail in chapter 4. Jonah 1:17, Matthew 27:63, and other similar verses refer to the crucifixion and resurrection of Jesus Christ. He was crucified and was resurrected on the third day.

4 = Creative Works

- Exodus 25:12 - "You shall cast four rings of gold for it, and put them in the four corners thereof; and two rings shall be in one side of it, and two rings in the other side of it [KJV]."
- Exodus 25:26 - "You shall make for it four rings of gold, and put the rings in the four corners that are on the four feet thereof [KJV]."
- Exodus 25:34 - "And in the candlesticks shall be four bowls made like unto almonds, with their knobs and their flowers [KJV]."
- Leviticus 11:20,21 - "All fowls that creep, going upon all four, shall be an abomination unto you. Yet these may you eat of every flying creeping thing that goes upon all four, which have legs above their feet, to leap withal upon the

earth [KJV]."
- Job 1:19 - "Behold, there came a great wind from the wilderness, and smote the four corners of the house, and it fell upon the young men, and they are dead; and I only am escaped alone to tell you [KJV]."
- Isaiah 11:12 - "He shall set up an ensign (banner) for the nations, and shall assemble the outcasts of Israel, and gather together the dispersed of Judah from the four corners of the earth [KJV]."
- Jeremiah 15:3 - "'I will appoint over them four kinds,' says the Lord: 'the sword to slay, and the dogs to tear, and the fowls of the heaven, and the beasts of the earth, to devour and destroy' [KJV]."
- Ezekiel 1:5,6,8 - "Out of the midst thereof came the likeness of four living creatures. And this was their appearance; they had the likeness of a man. And every one had four faces, and every one had four wings. And they had the hands of a man under their wings on their four sides; and they four had their faces and their wings [KJV]."
- Daniel 7:6 - "After this I beheld, and lo another, like a leopard, which had upon the back of it four wings of a fowl; the beast had also four heads; and dominion was given to it [KJV]."
- Daniel 7:17 - "These great beasts, which are four, are four kings, which shall arise out of the earth [KJV]."
- Revelation 4:6,7 - "Before the throne there was a sea of glass like unto crystal: and in the midst of the throne, and round about the throne, were four beasts full of eyes before and behind. And the first beast was like a lion, and the second beast like a calf, and the third beast had a face as a man, and

the fourth beast was like a flying eagle [KJV]."

Four is used 421 times in the New King James Version of the Bible. When it is not used to reference a specific number, it is used symbolically to represent created entities. The phrase "four corners of the earth" represents all directions. Some prophecies, such as Ezekiel 1 and Daniel 7, represent specific kings or kingdoms (i.e. King Nebuchadnezzar of the Babylonian Empire, Cyrus the Great of the Medo-Persian Empire, Alexander the Great of the Greek Empire, and Julius Caesar of the Roman Empire - see Chapter 5).

Something that needs to be given some context is when the Bible says that insects (fowls that creep) have four legs or crawl on all fours. According to modern science, insects have six legs. The Bible differentiates between the front two pairs of legs and the back pair of legs. In insects, such as grasshoppers and locusts, the hind legs are built for jumping and leaping. They look very different than the front four legs. When the Bible says "all fours," it is only referencing the front four legs.

5 = God's Grace, Generosity, and Goodness

- Genesis 43:34 - "He took and sent messes (servings) unto them from before him: but Benjamin's mess was five times so much as any of their's. And they drank, and were merry with him [KJV]."
- Genesis 45:22 - "To all of them he gave each man changes of raiment (clothing); but to Benjamin he gave three hundred pieces of silver, and five changes of raiment [KJV]."
- Exodus 26:3 - "The five curtains shall be coupled together one to another; and other five curtains shall be coupled one

to another [KJV]."
- Exodus 26:26,27 - "You shall make bars of shittim (acacia) wood; five for the boards of the one side of the tabernacle, and five bars for the boards of the other side of the tabernacle, and five bars for the boards of the side of the tabernacle, for the two sides westward [KJV]."
- Exodus 26:37 - "You shall make for the hanging five pillars of shittim (acacia) wood, and overlay them with gold, and their hooks shall be of gold: and you shall cast five sockets of brass for them [KJV]."
- 1 Samuel 21:3 - "Now therefore what is under your hand? Give me five loaves of bread in my hand, or what there is present [KJV]."
- 1 Kings 7:39 - "He put five bases on the right side of the house, and five on the left side of the house: and he set the sea on the right side of the house eastward over against the south [KJV]."
- 1 Kings 7:49 - "the candlesticks of pure gold, five on the right side, and five on the left, before the oracle, with the flowers, and the lamps, and the tongs of gold [KJV]."
- Matthew 16:9 - "Do you not yet understand, neither remember the five loaves of the five thousand, and how many baskets you took up [KJV]?"
- Luke 12:6 - "Are not five sparrows sold for two farthings (copper coins), and not one of them is forgotten before God [KJV]?"
- 2 Corinthians 11:24 - "Of the Jews five times received I forty stripes save one [KJV]."

Five is used 275 times in the New King James Version of the Bible.

The feeding of the 5000 by Jesus is the only miracle, other than His resurrection, recorded in all four Gospels (Matthew 14, Mark 6, Luke 9, John 6). It is important to note that this miracle took place during the second Passover of the ministry of Jesus (John 6:4) (see Chapter 4). The second feeding miracle, the feeding of the 4000, is told in Matthew 15 and Mark 8 and is linked to the feeding of the 5000. These stories capture the essential truth about God's purpose, Jesus' mission, and His disciples. In the first event, they were given five barley loaves and two fish. After the multitudes were fed, there were twelve baskets of leftovers. In the second event, the disciples had seven loaves of bread and a few fish. After the multitudes were fed, there were seven baskets of leftovers. These events collectively demonstrate His grace, generosity, and good works. The Feast of Unleavened Bread, the feeding of the 5000, and the Last Supper all point to the redemptive work of Jesus Christ.

6 = Man, Man's Government

- Exodus 20:9 - "Six days shall you shall labor, and do all your work [KJV]."
- Exodus 21:2 - "If you buy a Hebrew servant, six years he shall serve: and in the seventh he shall go out free for nothing [KJV]."
- Exodus 24:16 - "The glory of the Lord abode upon Mount Sinai, and the cloud covered it six days: and the seventh day He called unto Moses out of the midst of the cloud [KJV]."
- Exodus 25:32 - "Six branches shall come out of the sides of it; three branches of the candlestick out of the one side, and three branches of the candlestick out of the other side [KJV]."
- Numbers 35:6 - "Among the cities which you shall give unto

- the Levites there shall be six cities for refuge, which you shall appoint for the manslayer, that he may flee thither (to that place): and to them you shall add forty and two cities [KJV]."
- 1 Kings 10:19 - "The throne had six steps, and the top of the throne was round behind: and there were stays (armrests) on either side on the place of the seat, and two lions stood beside the stays [KJV]."
- Job 5:19 - "He shall deliver you in six troubles: yea, in seven there shall no evil touch you [KJV]."
- Revelation 4:8 - "The four beasts had each of them six wings about him; and they were full of eyes within: and they rest not day and night, saying, 'Holy, holy, holy, Lord God Almighty, which was, and is, and is to come' [KJV]."
- Revelation 13:18 - "Here is wisdom. Let him that has understanding count the number of the beast: for it is the number of a man; and his number is Six hundred threescore and six (666) [KJV]."

Six is used 317 times in the New King James Version of the Bible, and 666 is used once. Man was created on the sixth day, and we are appointed to work six days and rest for one day. Six cities of refuge were given to the Levites (Numbers 35:6). God established these cities so that others would not retaliate against those who inflicted bodily harm on others. The number six represents mankind and mankind's system of government. Man is incomplete and imperfect without God.

The number 666 is a special case. Revelation 13 describes three separate personalities. Some people have labeled them the "Unholy Trinity": The Dragon, the Beast, and the False Prophet. The Dragon is Satan. He has been fighting against Jesus for dominion of the world since before the time of Genesis 3. The Beast or the Antichrist is a man spiritually aligned with Satan. He will become the leader of the world during the end times. The False Prophet will seem gentle, but will deceive and speak evil. He will perform great signs and force people to worship an image of the Antichrist.

7 = Spiritual Completeness, Spiritual Perfection

- Genesis 2:2,3 - "On the seventh day God ended His work which He had made; and He rested on the seventh day from all His work which He had made. And God blessed the seventh day, and sanctified it: because that in it He had rested from all His work which God created and made [KJV]."
- Genesis 4:15 - "The Lord said unto him, 'Therefore whosoever slays Cain, vengeance shall be taken on him sevenfold.' And the Lord set a mark upon Cain, lest any finding him should kill him [KJV]."
- Genesis 4:24 - "If Cain shall be avenged sevenfold, truly Lamech seventy and sevenfold [KJV]."
- Genesis 7:2-4 - "Of every clean beast you shall take to you by sevens, the male and his female; and of beasts that are not clean by two, the male and his female. Of fowls also of the air by sevens, the male and the female, to keep seed alive upon the face of all the earth. For yet seven days, and I will cause it to rain upon the earth forty days and forty nights; and every living substance that I have made will I destroy from off the face of the earth [KJV]."
- Genesis 21:28-30 - "Abraham set seven ewe lambs of the flock by themselves. And Abimelech said unto Abraham, 'What mean these seven ewe lambs which you have set by themselves?' And he said, 'For these seven ewe lambs shall

you take of my hand, that they may be a witness unto me, that I have dug this well' [KJV]."

- Exodus 12:15 - "Seven days shall you eat unleavened bread, even the first day you shall put away leaven out of your houses: for whosoever eats leavened bread from the first day until the seventh day, that soul shall be cut off from Israel [KJV]."
- Job 5:19 - "He shall deliver you in six troubles; yea, in seven there shall no evil touch you [KJV]."
- Psalm 12:6 - "The words of the Lord are pure words, as silver tried in a furnace of earth, purified seven times [KJV]."
- Psalm 119:164 - "Seven times a day do I praise You because of Your righteous judgments [KJV]."
- Ezekiel 40:26 - "There were seven steps to go up to it, and the arches thereof were before them; and it had palm trees, one on this side, and another on that side, upon the posts thereof [KJV]."
- Zechariah 4:2 - "And said unto me, 'What do you see?' And I said, 'I have looked, and behold a candlestick all of gold, with a bowl upon the top of it, and his seven lamps thereon, and seven pipes to the seven lamps, which are upon the top thereof' [KJV]."
- Matthew 15:34,36,37 - "Jesus said unto them, 'How many loaves do you have?' And they said, 'Seven, and a few little fish.' And He took the seven loaves and the fish, and gave thanks, and broke them, and gave to His disciples, and the disciples to the multitude. And they did all eat, and were filled; and they took up of the broken meat that was left seven baskets full [KJV]."
- Revelation 1:11 - "Saying, 'I am Alpha and the Omega, the

First and the Last,' and, 'What you see, write in a book, and send it unto the seven churches which are in Asia; unto Ephesus, and unto Smyrna, and unto Pergamos, and unto Thyatira, and unto Sardis, and unto Philadelphia, and unto Laodicea' [KJV]."
- Revelation 1:20 - "The mystery of the seven stars which you have seen in my right hand, and the seven golden candlesticks. The seven stars are the angels of the seven churches: and the seven candlesticks which you have seen are the seven churches [KJV]."
- Revelation 5:1 - "I saw in the right hand of him that sat on the throne a book written within and on the backside, sealed with seven seals [KJV]."
- Revelation 5:6 - "I beheld, and, lo, in the midst of the throne and of the four beasts, and in the midst of the elders, stood a Lamb as it had been slain, having seven horns and seven eyes, which are the seven Spirits of God sent forth into all the earth [KJV]."

Seven is used 603 times in the New King James Version of the Bible. God rested on the 7th day of creation and made it holy (Genesis 2). Seven represents spiritual completeness and permeates the entire Bible. 7 ewe lambs are referenced in Genesis 21, and 7 churches are mentioned in Revelation 1. There is often an effort or action associated with the number. God worked for six days and rested on the seventh day. Israel quietly walked around the city of Jericho once a day for six days and seven times on the seventh day (Joshua 6). Jesus fed 4000 with seven loaves of bread and seven baskets were left over (Matthew 15). There is a difference between the number three and the number seven in the Bible. Where 7 represents an action, 3 typically represents a state of being. Three represents the divinity of

God, whereas seven represents the spiritual efforts of God. There are three special cases of the number seven: 21, 77, and 777. These three numbers will be discussed in more detail in chapter 6.

10 = Law, Testimony, Obedience

- Genesis 24:55 - "Her brother and her mother said, 'Let the damsel abide with us a few days, at the least ten; after that she shall go' [KJV]."
- Exodus 26:1 - "You shall make the tabernacle with ten curtains of fine twined linen, and blue, and purple, and scarlet: with cherubims of cunning work shall you make them [KJV]."
- Exodus 27:12 - "For the breadth of the court on the west side shall be hangings of fifty cubits: their pillars ten, and their sockets ten [KJV]."
- Exodus 34:28 - "He was there with the Lord forty days and forty nights; he did neither eat bread, nor drink water. And he wrote upon the tables the words of the covenant, the Ten Commandments [KJV]."
- 2 Chronicles 4:6-8 - "He made also ten lavers (basins), and put five on the right hand, and five on the left, to wash in them: such things as they offered for the burnt offering they washed in them; but the sea was for the priests to wash in. And he made ten candlesticks of gold according to their form, and set them in the temple, five on the right hand, and five on the left. He made also ten tables, and placed them in the temple, five on the right side, and five on the left. And he made a hundred basins of gold [KJV]."
- Matthew 25:1 - "Then shall the kingdom of heaven be

likened unto ten virgins, which took their lamps, and went forth to meet the bridegroom [KJV]."

Ten is used 280 times in the New King James Version of the Bible. It is most closely associated with the Ten Commandments. These commandments given to Moses became the foundation for all the other laws associated with the nation of Israel. Their purpose is associated with the restoration of man's relationship with God and with each other. Matthew 22:37-39 states, "Jesus said unto him, 'You shall love the Lord your God with all your heart, and with all your soul, and with all your mind. This is the first and great commandment. And the second is like unto it, you shall love your neighbor as yourself [KJV]." We demonstrate our love for and faith in God by being obedient to these commandments.

Paul writes in Galatians 3:19-24, "What purpose then serves the law? It was added because of transgressions, till the seed should come to whom the promise was made; and it was ordained by angels in the hand of a mediator. Now a mediator is not a mediator of one, but God is one. Is the law then against the promises of God? God forbid: for if there had been a law given which could have given life, verily righteousness should have been by the law. But the scripture has concluded all under sin, that the promise by faith of Jesus Christ might be given to them that believe. But before faith came, we were kept under the law, shut up unto the faith which should afterwards be revealed. Wherefore the law was our schoolmaster to bring us unto Christ, that we might be justified by faith [KJV]."

If the Ten Commandments and the Law were not there to provide salvation, then why were they given to us by God through Moses? Many have believed that if they kept the law, they would earn salvation and eternal life with God. Ephesians 2:8-9 states, "For by grace are you saved through faith; and that not of yourselves: it is the gift of God: not of works, lest any man should boast [KJV]." Paul makes it very clear that salvation is not through good works, but that it is through the grace of God. It is not anything we can earn. It is a free gift from God.

The purpose of the Law is twofold. First, God instituted laws and governance to maintain civil order. We are broken and sinful. The Bible clearly states those actions which need to be punished, it also describes the necessary punishments. Deuteronomy 15 allowed for indentured servitude. People would voluntarily give their labor for free in order to pay off debts or to secure food and shelter. The chapter also clearly describes how to treat this servant. At the end of six years, the servant would go free and share in the fruits of his/her labor.

The second purpose of the Law is spiritual in nature. The Law clearly defines what sin is. To be sinless is to never break any of the Ten Commandments. The Law acts as a hammer convicting us of our own sinful nature. When Jesus died for our sins when He was sinless, He took on all our sins and became the conduit for us to have a relationship with God. The Law also points us in the direction of God's grace, which is the only way we can be saved.

The Ten Commandments demonstrate God's desire to restore us (His saints) to Him. Our righteous acts as followers of Christ as illuminated by the Ten Commandments are not a path to Heaven, but these commandments show the way. Our salvation is a free gift from God that cannot be earned. We show obedience to the Law because we have faith and trust in God's promises.

12 = Discipleship, Faith

- Genesis 14:4 - "Twelve years they served Chedorlaomer, and in the thirteenth year they rebelled [KJV]."
- Genesis 17:20 - "As for Ishmael, I have heard you: Behold, I have blessed him, and will make him fruitful, and will multiply him exceedingly; twelve princes shall he beget, and I will make him a great nation [KJV]."
- Genesis 35:22 - " It came to pass, when Israel dwelt in that land, that Reuben went and lay with Bilhah his father's concubine: and Israel heard it. Now the sons of Jacob were twelve [KJV]."
- Numbers 7:84,86,87 - "This was the dedication of the altar, in the day when it was anointed, by the princes of Israel: twelve chargers of silver, twelve silver bowls, twelve spoons of gold... The golden spoons were twelve, full of incense, weighing ten shekels apiece, after the shekel of the sanctuary: all the gold of the spoons was a hundred and twenty shekels. All the oxen for the burnt offering were twelve bullocks, the rams twelve, the lambs of the first year twelve, with their meat offering: and the kids of the goats for sin offering twelve [KJV]."
- Matthew 10:1,2,5 - "When he had called unto him his twelve disciples, he gave them power against unclean spirits, to cast them out, and to heal all manner of sickness and all manner of disease. Now the names of the twelve apostles are these; The first, Simon, who is called Peter, and Andrew his brother; James the son of Zebedee, and John his brother... These twelve Jesus sent forth, and commanded them, saying, 'Go not into the way of the Gentiles, and into any city of the Samaritans enter ye not' [KJV]."

- Matthew 14:20 - "They did all eat, and were filled: and they took up of the fragments that remained twelve baskets full [KJV]."
- Matthew 19:28 - "Jesus said unto them, 'Verily I say unto you, That you which have followed me, in the regeneration when the Son of man shall sit in the throne of His glory, you also shall sit upon twelve thrones, judging the twelve tribes of Israel' [KJV]."
- Revelation 12:1 - "There appeared a great wonder in heaven; a woman clothed with the sun, and the moon under her feet, and upon her head a crown of twelve stars [KJV]."
- Revelation 21:12,14,21 - "And had a wall great and high, and had twelve gates, and at the gates twelve angels, and names written thereon, which are the names of the twelve tribes of the children of Israel... And the wall of the city had twelve foundations, and in them the names of the twelve apostles of the Lamb... And the twelve gates were twelve pearls: every several gate was of one pearl: and the street of the city was pure gold, as it were transparent glass [KJV]."
- Revelation 22:2 - "In the midst of the street of it, and on either side of the river, was there the tree of life, which bare twelve manner of fruits, and yielded her fruit every month: and the leaves of the tree were for the healing of the nations [KJV]."

Twelve is used 165 times in the New King James Version of the Bible. There are twelve sons of Israel in the Old Testament and twelve disciples of Jesus in the New Testament. Revelation 21 mentions both of these groups in the context of New Jerusalem. Only those who are entered into the Book of Life are allowed to enter the city. Jesus had not yet fulfilled His mission in the time of the tribes of Israel and the Old Testament. Those who had faith in the promises of the Law and the Prophets during this time were written into the Book of Life. The Church Age began after the resurrection and ascension of Jesus Christ. Those who have faith in the promises of Jesus Christ during this time are written into the Book of Life.

40 = Trials

- Genesis 7:4 - "For yet seven days, and I will cause it to rain upon the earth forty days and forty nights; and every living substance that I have made will I destroy from off the face of the earth [KJV]."
- Exodus 16:35 - "The children of Israel did eat manna forty years, until they came to a land inhabited; they did eat manna, until they came unto the borders of the land of Canaan [KJV]."
- Exodus 24:18 - "Moses went into the midst of the cloud, and went up into the mount: and Moses was in the mount forty days and forty nights [KJV]."
- Exodus 26:19 - "You shall make forty sockets of silver under the twenty boards; two sockets under one board for his two tenons, and two sockets under another board for his two tenons [KJV]."
- Exodus 34:28 - "He was there with the Lord forty days and forty nights; he did neither eat bread, nor drink water. And he wrote upon the tables the words of the covenant, the Ten Commandments [KJV]."
- Numbers 13:25 - "They returned from searching of the land after forty days [KJV]."

- Numbers 14:34 - "After the number of the days in which you searched the land, even forty days, each day for a year, shall you bear your iniquities, even forty years, and you shall know my breach of promise [KJV]."
- Deuteronomy 8:2,4 - "You shall remember all the way which the Lord your God led you these forty years in the wilderness, to humble you, and to prove you, to know what was in your heart, whether you would keep His commandments, or no... Your raiment waxed not old upon you, neither did your foot swell, these forty years [KJV]."
- Deuteronomy 9:9,11 - "When I was gone up into the mount to receive the tables of stone, even the tables of the covenant which the Lord made with you, then I abode in the mount forty days and forty nights, I neither did eat bread nor drink water... And it came to pass at the end of forty days and forty nights, that the Lord gave me the two tables of stone, even the tables of the covenant [KJV]."
- Deuteronomy 25:3 - "Forty stripes he may give him, and not exceed: lest, if he should exceed, and beat him above these with many stripes, then your brother should seem vile unto you [KJV]."
- Mark 1:13 - "He was there in the wilderness forty days, tempted of Satan; and was with the wild beasts; and the angels ministered unto Him [KJV]."

Forty is used 147 times in the New King James Version of the Bible. There is a consistent theme throughout the Bible associated with this number. During the Genesis Flood, it rained for 40 days and 40 nights. Israel wondered in the wilderness for 40 years. Jesus was tempted by Satan for 40 days. It is both literal and symbolic of a time of testing and trials. As followers of Christ, we will face trials of our faith. It is not about a separation from God. It's the exact opposite. It is during this time of trials that we are to draw closer to Him, to learn from Him, and to find strength in His presence. This is discussed more in Chapter 6.

Chapter 4

Seven Feasts

"Six days may work be done; but in the seventh is the Sabbath of rest, holy to the Lord: whosoever does any work in the Sabbath day, he shall surely be put to death [KJV]."
- Exodus 31:15

Leviticus 23 sums up the critical work of Jesus Christ as described through the establishment of seven feasts: Passover, Unleavened Bread, First fruits, Weeks, Trumpets, Atonement, and Tabernacles. This chapter describes what these feasts are and delves into their meanings, what Moses wrote about them, and what they mean about our relationship with Jesus Christ.

Hebrew Calendar

Just as we celebrate New Year's Day on January 1 every year, Jews celebrate the Feast of Trumpets or Rosh Hashanah (their New Year's Day) on the 1st day of Tishri every year. It is helpful to understand how the Hebrew calculate time in order to better understand its culture and important dates within the Bible.

This next part is a little complicated. We will try to explain it as clearly as possible. The Hebrew calendar is based on three astronomical phenomena: the rotation of the Earth around its axis (a day), the revolution of the Moon around the Earth (a month), and the revolution of the Earth around the Sun (a year). The Moon revolves around the Earth about every 29½ days. The Earth revolves around the Sun about every 365.242 days or 12.4 months. To accommodate for the extra 0.242 days or 0.4 months, we need to modify the calendar occasionally. In modern solar calendars, we add an extra day once every four years. This is called Leap Year. We add February 29 to the calendar once every four years. The way the Hebrew managed the partial month is to add a leap month (or a 13th month) once every few years. Even with these adjustments, the conversion between the Hebrew Lunar calendar and the Roman solar calendar is off by 0.008 or about 1 day every 128 years. For short-term calculations, this difference is minor. However, in time calculations that span hundreds or thousands of years, these differences can cause calendar synchronizations to be off by days or possibly weeks. With this in mind, conversions between the Hebrew Lunar calendar and Roman Solar calendar may be off by a few days.

The modern civil calendar used by most of the world, which is strongly influenced by the Roman solar calendar, has abandoned any use of Moon cycles arbitrarily setting the length of months to 28, 29, 30, or 31 days. Solar cycles start over on January 1 just after the winter solstice in the Northern Hemisphere (i.e. December 21). The Hebrew lunar cycles start over in the spring just before Passover.

Special note: Hebrews used 360 days / year instead of 365¼ days / year in certain long-term calculations related to prophecies. This prophetic year is used in the Book of Daniel (see Chapter 5).

Promise Keeper

Hebrew Months

#	Hebrew	Length	Civil Equivalent
1	Nisan	30 days	March-April
2	Iyar / Ziv	29 days	April-May
3	Sivan	30 days	May-June
4	Tammuz	29 days	June-July
5	Av	30 days	July-August
6	Elul	29 days	August-September
7	Tishri	30 days	September-October
8	Cheshvan	29-30 days	October-November
9	Kislev	29-30 days	November-December
10	Tevet	29 days	December-January
11	Shevat	30 days	January-February
12	Adar	30 days	February-March

Leap Years Only:
| 12 | Adar I | 30 days |
| 13 | Adar II | 29 days |

Hebrew Days of the Week

Yom Rishon = First Day = Sunday
Yom Sheini = Second Day = Monday
Yom Shlishi = Third Day = Tuesday
Yom R'vi'i = Fourth Day = Wednesday
Yom Chamishi = Fifth Day = Thursday
Yom Shishi = Sixth Day = Friday
Yom Shabbat = Seventh Day = Saturday

Dates of the Feasts

Based on specific descriptions within the Bible, the seven feasts are on the dates listed below:

Passover	Nisan 14
Unleavened Bread	Nisan 15 – 21
Firstfruits	Nisan 17
Weeks	Sivan 6
Trumpets	Tishri 1
Atonement	Tishri 10
Tabernacles	Tishri 15 - 21

Passover / Pesach

The tenth plague that struck against Egypt during the time of Exodus was that of the death of the firstborn child in every home (Exodus 12). God instructed the Israelites through Moses and Aaron to follow specific instructions in order to prevent the Israelites from this calamity. The following is an edited version of those instructions:

<u>Exodus 12: 2-3, 5-7, 12-13, 43, 46-47, 50-51</u>

"(2) This month shall be unto you the beginning of months: it shall be the first month of the year to you. (3) Speak unto all the congregation of Israel, saying, 'In the tenth day of this month they shall take to them every man a lamb, according to the house of their fathers, a lamb for an house... (5) Your lamb shall be without blemish, a male of the first year: you shall take it out from the sheep, or from the goats: (6) And you shall keep it up until the fourteenth day of the same month: and the whole assembly of the congregation of Israel shall kill it in the evening. (7) And they shall take of the blood, and strike it on the two side posts and on the upper door post of the houses, wherein they shall eat it... (12) For I will pass through the land of Egypt this night, and will smite all the firstborn in the land of Egypt, both man and beast; and against all the gods of Egypt I will execute judgment: I am the Lord. (13) And the blood shall be to you for a token upon the houses where you are: and when I see the blood, I will pass over you, and the plague shall not be upon you to destroy you, when I smite the land of Egypt...' (43) And the Lord said unto Moses and Aaron, 'This is the ordinance of the Passover: There shall no stranger eat thereof... (46) In one house shall it be eaten; you shall not carry forth ought of the flesh abroad out of the house; neither shall you break a bone thereof.' (47) All the congregation of Israel shall keep it... (50) Thus did all the children of Israel; as the Lord commanded Moses and Aaron, so did they. (51) And it came to pass the selfsame day, that the Lord did bring the children of Israel out of the land of Egypt by their armies [KJV]."

<u>Jesus the Messiah as the Passover Lamb</u>

The Book of Exodus describes how Moses was sent by God to Pharaoh to be a deliverer of Israel. Pharaoh did not set the people of Israel free, which set the stage for God's triumph over Egypt. The tenth and final plague descended upon the people of Egypt, which was the death of the firstborn sons in the land. Only those families that sacrificed an unblemished lamb and smeared its blood upon the doorposts of the house would be "passed over" from the impending wrath of God. On Nisan 10 each head of the household set aside a young flawless male lamb. This period allowed each family to become personally attached to its lamb. On the afternoon of Nisan 14 the lambs were to be publicly sacrificed. Even though the entire nation of Israel was responsible for the death of the lambs, each family was to individually apply the blood of its personal lamb upon the doorpost as a sign of faith in God's deliverance.

After Jesus the Messiah was crucified, the Temple was destroyed (70 AD) and Rabbinical Judaism eventually assumed leadership of the Jewish people. According to the rabbis, the idea of blood sacrifice was changed to mean prayer and the following of Rabbinical law. The rabbis then decreed that Passover should be commemorated by means of the Passover Seder, held on Nisan 15. Technically speaking, Passover is a one day festival that commemorates God's deliverance from Egypt and is immediately followed by the seven-day Feast of Unleavened Bread. Modern Judaism, however, considers Passover to be an eight-day holiday that remembers the birth of the Jewish people as a nation under the leadership of Moses. For Christians and Messianic Jews, the Passover is a day of remembrance for the sacrifice of Jesus the Messiah as the Lamb of God who takes away the sins of the world. This is the real meaning of Passover. It is therefore no coincidence that Jesus was crucified on Passover as the perfect sacrificial lamb (Mark 14:1).

Feast of Unleavened Bread / Chag HaMatzot

Deuteronomy 16:3 states, "You shall eat no leavened bread with it; seven days shall you eat unleavened bread therewith, even the bread of affliction; for you came forth out of the land of Egypt in haste: that you may remember the day when you came forth out of the land of Egypt all the days of your life [KJV]." As described earlier, this week-long feast occurs between Nisan 15 and 21. What is the role of matzah (unleavened bread) and the Feast of Unleavened Bread? How is this fulfilled in the ministry of Jesus?

Leaven (yeast) produces fermentation, especially in bread dough, and is the result of natural processes of decay. According to the Bible (Exodus 13:7, Deuteronomy 16:4), all leaven must be removed from where you live. So what is the problem with leaven? It is a symbol of decay. The "rise of dough" is only made possible by the natural processes of converting sugar to ethyl alcohol and carbon dioxide. Leaven is used as a symbol for sin. 1 Corinthians 5:7-8 encourages us to: "Purge out therefore the old leaven, that you may be a new lump, as you are unleavened. For even Christ our Passover is sacrificed for us: Therefore let us keep the feast, not with old leaven, neither with the leaven of malice and wickedness; but with the unleavened bread of sincerity and truth [KJV]."

Unleavened bread is a picture of holiness, purity, and sinlessness. Jesus' life and sacrifice was without the taint of the curse of death. Jesus was buried on Nisan 15. After He was buried, He did not suffer the natural process of corruption (decomposition). His body did not return to dust as was Adam's fate as described in Genesis 3:19. As the Second Adam, His sacrifice removed the power of death (Hebrews 9:26).

Sanctification is a work of the Holy Spirit in our lives (1 Corinthians 6:11). We become sanctified by sincerely trusting in the afflictions that Jesus endured on our behalf. Just as we are saved by God's grace through faith, so are we also sanctified. It is not earned through deeds (Titus 3:5). It is freely given to those who humble themselves and trust in Jesus the Messiah (John 6:29). Unleavened bread, then, signifies our identification with Jesus in his humility, afflictions, and sacrifice.

Feast of Firstfruits / Reshit Katzir

The day following the first day of the Feast of Unleavened Bread is called Reshit Katzir (Beginning of the Harvest). It occurs on Nisan 17. It is not by accident that Moses parted the Red Sea to escape Pharaoh's army on Nisan 17 (Exodus 13-14). Let's look at that statement more closely.

Nisan 14: Passover lamb to be killed at twilight (Exodus 12:6).
Nisan 15: Israelites leave Egypt (Exodus 12:51, 13:3).
Nisan 16: Israelites camp near Pi Hahiroth (Exodus 14:1).
Nisan 17: Moses parts the Red Sea (Exodus 14:13).

<u>Nisan 17 Events in the Bible</u>

Many significant Biblical events occurred on Nisan 17.

- Noah's Ark rested on the mountains of Ararat after the Great Flood (Genesis 8:4, Exodus 12:2).
- Moses parted the Red Sea (Exodus 14:13).
- The manna which had fed the people of Israel for the 40 years in the wilderness stopped on the 16th of Nisan. From the 17th onward Israel feasted on the new grain of the Promised Land (Joshua 5:10-12).
- Esther proclaimed a three day fast (Esther 4:16) for the 14th, 15th, and 16th. On Nisan 17, the Jews were saved and the enemy hung.
- Seven sons of Saul were hung which represents a victory for David (2 Samuel 21).
- Nehemiah viewed the destroyed wall of Jerusalem and encouraged its rebuilding (Nehemiah 2).
- Jesus was resurrected on Nisan 17 (Luke 24:1-7).

Jesus As the Firstfruits

1 Corinthians 15:20-23 states that Jesus has risen from the dead and has become the first fruits to those who have fallen asleep. The Feast of Firstfruits represents the resurrection of Jesus Christ. When God raised Jesus from the dead, He absolved Jesus of the sins He bore, and those who believe in Him and the true power of His sacrifice. Those that believe will also be pardoned and have everlasting life (John 3:16).

Feast of Weeks / Shavuot

Exodus 34:22 states, "You shall observe the Feast of Weeks, of the firstfruits of wheat harvest, and the Feast of Ingathering at the year's end [KJV]." Unlike Passover, which is mentioned over 80 times in the Bible, the Feast of Weeks is only mentioned 5 times. Leviticus 23:15 and Deuteronomy 16:9 mention that the Feast of Weeks is to be celebrated 7 weeks after the first Sabbath following Passover. This would be 50 days after Passover or 49 days after the first Sabbath (Feast of Unleavened Bread). This by itself is not much to go on. However, this feast is quite often associated with the wheat harvest. If we expand our search of the Bible to include this term, we get a little clearer message as to the importance of this feast. There are 9 references to wheat harvest in the Bible. We would like to focus on three of them: Judges 15:1, Ruth 2:23, and 1 Samuel 6:13.

Samson Defeats the Philistines (Judges 15)

This chapter is about Samson, a judge of Israel, his wife, and his wife's father. It occurred during the time of the wheat harvest. Samson's wife was a Philistine – an ungodly non-Hebrew woman.

Even though he had an unsympathetic relationship with his father-in-law, the real root of the problem is that he made bad choices in whom he had a romantic relationship with. Even though Samson was imperfect, God was still able to use Samson for His purpose. Samson caught three hundred foxes (which could also be translated as jackals), attached fire to them, and set them loose to burn the Philistine's fields. Soon after, 3000 of his own men came to capture him and take him to the Philistines. He was bound by two new pieces of rope and taken to the Philistines. He let them because of their promise that none of them would harm him. The fact that soldiers from the tribe of Judah gave Samson up to the Philistines (which parallels the Jews who gave Jesus up to Roman leadership) demonstrates that they would rather please their oppressors than support their deliverer. When they arrived at a Philistine encampment, Samson was loosed by God, grabbed the jawbone of a donkey, and killed a thousand men. After this he became thirsty, so God split a hollow place and water came out [Judges 15:19].

Ruth and Boaz (Book of Ruth)

The story of Ruth is that of an ordinary woman from from the small nation of Moab who ends up doing extraordinary things. There was a famine in Israel, so Elimelech (whose name means "My God Is King") moved Naomi (his wife) and his family from Bethlehem to Moab, which is a nation that did not worship the God of Abraham and Isaac. Elimelech's family lived there for ten years and his sons married local women (Orpah and Ruth). The father and the two sons died. Also, neither Orpah or Ruth had any sons. Orpah stayed in Moab. Naomi and Ruth returned to Judah. Ruth said this to Naomi:

"Entreat me not to leave you,
Or to return from following after you:
For whither you go, I will go;
And where you lodge, I will lodge:
Your people shall be my people,
And your God, my God:
Where you die, I will die,
And there will I be buried:
The Lord do so to me, and more also,
If ought but death part you and me [Ruth 1:16-17 KJV]."

Ruth was ready to give up everything in order to stay with Naomi and go to Judah. They reached Bethlehem at the beginning of the barley harvest (Ruth 1:22), which is around the time of the Feast of Weeks. Ruth went to the fields to get food. She happened to go to the fields owned by Boaz, who was an honorable man of great wealth and related to Elimelech (Ruth 2:1). Leviticus 19:9-10 states that a portion of the harvest shall be made available to the poor and the stranger. As a result, Ruth could "glean" from Boaz's fields without issue. Boaz found out about Ruth and Naomi and said this to Ruth, "Go not to glean in another field, neither go from here, but abide here fast by my maidens: Let your eyes be on the field that they do reap, and go after them [Ruth 2:8-9 KJV]." Ruth bowed down to Boaz and said, "Why have I found grace in your eyes, that you should take knowledge of me, seeing I am a stranger?... Let me find favor in your sight, my lord; for that you have comforted me, and for that you have spoken friendly unto your handmaid, though I be not like unto one of your handmaidens [Ruth 2:10,13 KJV]." Ruth continued to glean from the fields of Boaz until the end of the barley harvest [Ruth 2:23].

Boaz, aware that neither Naomi nor Ruth had any husband or son, took steps to reconcile it. Boaz talked to Naomi's closest relative that Naomi is selling a parcel of land that belonged to Elimelech. He encouraged the relative to purchase it and restore Naomi's and Ruth's family name. The closest relative passed on the offer, and Boaz was second in line for the purchase. Boaz purchased the land and restored their family name [Ruth 4].

Ruth means companion or friend. This, however, loses a bit in translation. This type of companion is much more than an acquaintance. She is steadfast, determined, resilient, and dedicated to be by your side. As a result of Ruth's steadfast companionship and Boaz's act of redemption, they had a son. His name was Obed (which means "servant"). He was the grandfather of King David.

Samuel and the Ark of the Covenant (1 Samuel 6)

The Ark of the Lord or the Ark of the Covenant was captured by the Philistines seven months earlier – which would have been some time in the previous autumn. Thinking it was a trophy of great victory, they soon realized the ark was a burden. The land was being ravaged by a plague. Based on the description in verse 4, it sounds like it might have been bubonic plague – also known as Black Death. It often causes boil like symptoms and is often transmitted by fleas from rats. The Philistine priests believed they had offended the God of the Israelites and decided to do something to rectify it. They were aware of the mistakes made by the Egyptian pharaohs and decided to send the Ark back to the Israelites. They placed it on a new cart along with some gold. They connected two milk cows that had never been yoked. Without any person directing them, the cows went directly towards the Israelite city of Beth Shemesh without stopping or moving off in another direction.

"They of Bethshemesh were reaping their wheat harvest in the valley: and they lifted up their eyes, and saw the ark, and rejoiced to see it. And the cart came into the field of Joshua, a Bethshemite, and stood there, where there was a great stone: and they clave (split) the wood of the cart, and offered the kine (cows) a burnt offering unto the Lord. And the Levites took down the ark of the Lord, and the coffer (chest) that was with it, wherein the jewels of gold were, and put them on the great stone: and the men of Bethshemesh offered burnt offerings and sacrificed sacrifices the same day unto the Lord [1 Samuel 6:13-15 KJV]."

Pentecost (Acts 2)

"When the Day of Pentecost (Feast of Weeks) was fully come, they were all with one accord in one place. And suddenly there came a sound from heaven as of a rushing mighty wind, and it filled all the house where they were sitting. And there appeared unto them cloven (divided) tongues like as of fire, and it sat upon each of them. And they were all filled with the Holy Ghost, and began to speak with other tongues, as the Spirit gave them utterance [Acts 2:1-4 KJV]."

As described above, the Feast of Weeks is about the event in which the Holy Spirit descended upon the Earth. As portrayed in Ruth, the Holy Spirit is a steadfast companion and redeemer. As seen with Samson and Ruth, He is able to use us in ways we may never think possible regardless of our background, status, or abilities. As seen in 1 Samuel, the Holy Spirit guides us.

The entire sequence of Passover, Unleavened Bread, Firstfruits, and

Weeks tells a singular story. Jesus was crucified as the perfect sacrificial lamb for our sins. He was buried and was resurrected on the third day. 40 days later, He ascended into heaven [Acts 1:3]. Seven weeks and one day after He was crucified, the Holy Spirit became our redeemer and companion.

There are two things mentioned in the three stories above that warrant further discussion. First, Judges 15:19 describes water coming out of a hollow place. The water coming out of a hollow space is a similar reference to Moses obtaining water from a rock in the desert (Numbers 20:11). Both of these are a reference to when Jesus died on the cross and water came from his side (John 19:34).

Second, Judges 15:13 mentions two new ropes, whereas 1 Samuel 6:7 mentions two milk cows that have never been yoked. The wheat harvest is mentioned in Judges 15:1 and 1 Samuel 6:13. The events of Judges 15 occurred about 20-25 years before King Saul was crowned. The events of 1 Samuel 6 occurred about 10-20 years before King Saul was crowned. These two passages mention the number two, something that is new, and someone or something that is tied up. They both occur at a time associated with the wheat harvest. Also, they probably don't occur the same year, but they do occur within about a decade of each other. Are there any symbolic comparisons between Sampson's ropes and the yoked cows? And if so what are they?

The stories of Ruth, Sampson, and Samuel referenced above are about the Holy Spirit being a helpful companion to us. It is possible that the number two in these stories references our union with the Holy Spirit as believers. 2 Corinthians 5:17 states, "Therefore if any man be in Christ, he is a new creature: old things are passed away;

behold, all things are become new [KJV]." The term "new" in both stories may be referencing this new creation. We can sum up the symbology of the three stories above as follows: Christ died for our sins. We who believe in Him are released from the bondage of sin and become new creatures. Meanwhile, the Holy Spirit comes alongside us and guides us on our journey in the direction God wants to take us.

Jubilee

49 is a number of significance within the Bible. As just mentioned, seven weeks and one day after Jesus was crucified, the Holy Spirit became our redeemer and companion. So, 49 is a representation of the Holy Spirit. There is a 49 year cycle described within the Bible. It is often referred to as a week of weeks or Jubilee.

"You shall number seven sabbaths of years unto you, seven times seven years; and the space of the seven sabbaths of years shall be unto you forty and nine years. Then shall you cause the trumpet of the Jubilee to sound on the tenth day of the seventh month, in the day of atonement shall you make the trumpet sound throughout all your land. And you shall hallow the fiftieth year, and proclaim liberty throughout all the land unto all the inhabitants thereof: it shall be a Jubilee unto you; and you shall return every man unto his possession, and you shall return every man unto his family. A Jubilee shall that fiftieth year be unto you: you shall not sow, neither reap that which grows of itself in it, nor gather the grapes in it of your vine undressed. For it is the Jubilee; it shall be holy unto you: you shall eat the increase thereof out of the field. In the year of this Jubilee you shall return every man unto his possession [Leviticus 25:8-13 KJV]."

According to the Bible, you shall count 49 years. The 50th year is a year of Jubilee. It is not coincidence that the 49+1 year cycle of Jubilee parallels the 49+1 days for Pentecost. Jubilee is a reminder of Pentecost or the arrival of the Holy Spirit after the crucifixion and ascension of Jesus Christ. There are three distinct features of the Jubilee Year: personal liberty, restitution of property, and rest. The 50th year was to be a time in which liberty should be proclaimed to all the inhabitants of the country. There shall be full restitution of all real property to the family which originally possessed it – this was a part of God's plan looking forward to the salvation of mankind. There shall also be a year of rest for the land – this was designed to remind us of our dependence on God.

Some major Biblical events occurred during years of Jubilee:

1406 BC – Crossed into Promised Land (Joshua 5)

According to Joshua 14:7, Joshua was 40 when he became a spy for Moses and entered the Promised Land for the first time. The nation disobeyed and they roamed the desert for 40 years. It was only at this time that the Israelites crossed the Jordan River under the leadership of Joshua and entered the land of Canaan. According to Joshua 24, Joshua lived 110 years. This would place his death in 1376 BC, and his birth in 1486 BC.

1308 BC – Judge Ehud killed King Eglon of Moab (Judges 3)

This may not have happened on the exact year of Jubilee, but time sequences put it either in or near 1308 BC. As a result of this event, Israel was freed from the tyranny of King Eglon and there was peace in the land.

1210 BC – Deborah became judge of Israel (Judges 4)

As with Judge Ehud, we do not know the exact year specific events took place, but we can deduce that Deborah became judge in or around 1210 BC. This was a time of great turmoil. The Bronze Age was coming to an end, and the Iron Age was making its presence known. Judges 4:3 describes 900 iron chariots. Under her leadership, Israel subdued its enemies, including King Jabin of Canaan, and brought peace to the land.

1162 BC – Gideon became a judge of Israel (Judges 6)
1063 BC - Philistines returned Ark (1 Samuel 6)

There is not a specific date for this event. This was shortly before Saul became king in 1052 BC. This event is probably associated with Jubilee. Jubilee is related to the Holy Spirit. It is very possible that this event occurred in a year of Jubilee.

1014 BC - David killed Philistines and escaped from King Saul (1 Samuel 19)

We do not know the exact year this event occurred, but based on chronology of events, it is possible that this took place in a year of Jubilee.

966 BC – King Solomon began First Temple (1 Kings 6)
869 BC – King Jehoshaphat succeeded King Asa (2 Chronicles 17)

King Jehoshaphat walked with God, whereas King Asa did not.

722 BC - Israel led into captivity (2 Kings 17)

2 Kings 17 describes why the Northern Kingdom was destroyed. They did evil things and turned away from God.

622 BC - Jeremiah proclaimed God's Covenant (Jeremiah 11, 12)
573 BC - Ezekiel received his vision on Nisan 10 (Ezekiel 40:1)

This vision was of a temple that was to be built some time in the future.

476 BC - Esther became queen (Esther 2)
64 AD – Herod's reconstruction of temple finished

There are two numbers that are used multiple times in the Bible. Both often reference specific amounts of time: 40 and 49. 40 represents a period of testing or probation. 49 represents liberty and rest. These two concepts play repeating roles within the stories of the Bible. We are faced with trials and tribulations. If we follow God's Word and rely on Him, we will find rest.

Feast of Trumpets / Rosh Hashanah

Leviticus 23:24 states, "In the seventh month, in the first day of the month, shall you have a sabbath, a memorial of blowing of trumpets, a holy convocation. [KJV]." The Feast of Trumpets, or Rosh Hashannah, is a celebration of the Jewish New Year. The holiday is observed on the first day of the Hebrew month of Tishri (i.e., the seventh "new moon" of the year), which falls between September 5 and October 5. It is celebrated with making loud sounds and blowing of trumpets. It is one of seven important feasts described in Leviticus, but it is not attached to any specific historical event. This has lead to much conjecture and guessing as to its significance. It may be associated with both the birth of Jesus and the rapture of the church upon His return. Below is a discussion of both ideas. Keep in mind that these next two sections are based more on best guesses rather than factual data.

Birth of Jesus

Traditionally, the birth of Jesus Christ is celebrated on December 25. This date was determined by Roman Emperor Lucius Aurelian (270-275 AD) in the third century AD. It was a celebration dedicated to the Sun God and associated with the winter solstice. He decreed that the followers of Christ could celebrate His birth on the same day. See Chapter 5 for the detailed discussion of Jesus' birth date.

By looking at the first advent of Jesus Christ, the feasts have significant meaning to His time on Earth. He died on Passover and was resurrected on the Feast of Firstfruits. The Holy Spirit descended to Earth during the Feast of Weeks. It would only be a very small leap of faith to assume that He was born on one of the seven feasts. The Day of Atonement is about forgiveness, and the Feast of Tabernacles is a multiple day festival related to the permanent establishment of God's kingdom. Passover, Unleavened Bread, Firstfruits, and Weeks have already been fulfilled. Also, they are in the spring and early summer. None of these are a good fit. The Feast of Trumpets is a fall feast and is about announcements. Trumpets were used for many things during this time, including directing troop movements and announcing a new king (1 Kings 1:34, 2 Kings 9:13, 2 Kings 11:11). As part of tradition, the Jews would already be shouting and blowing trumpets. This time they would be doing it to announce our newborn king.

There has been speculation for a while about a specific star and planet alignment at the birth of Jesus. We think that it is not clear enough to make any accurate statement, but nonetheless, one can interpret that the stars and planets were aligned a certain way on or around the day Jesus was born. The fact that wise men showed up from the East seeing a sign in the sky could be corroborating evidence for this [Matthew 2:1-2]. There is at least one possible explanation for this. Jupiter and Venus are the two brightest objects in the sky after the Sun and the Moon. These two planets have only crossed each other's path from our perspective four times in the last 2000 years. There was a Venus – Jupiter occultation visible from the Middle East at sunset on June 17, 2 BC. This corresponds to around Sivan 15 in the Hebrew calendar suggesting that there was also a full Moon that night. There was a solar eclipse a month and a half later July 31, 2 BC. This is very significant in that there is no other time within the past two thousand years that this type of arrangement occurred in the sky. We want to restate that this planet alignment may or may not be relevant. The Bible does not say one way or the other.

Rapture of the Church

Matthew 25:10 states, "While they went to buy, the bridegroom came; and they that were ready went in with him to the marriage: and the door was shut [KJV]." Also, Genesis 7:16 states this about Noah and the flood, "They that went in, went in male and female of all flesh, as God had commanded him: and the Lord shut him in [KJV]." Combining these stories, it is reasonable to conclude that Jesus will return without notice. We are to prepare for His return. Upon doing so, He will shut us away from the terrible events that occur next. When will He return?

1 Thessalonians 5:2 states, "For yourselves know perfectly that the day of the Lord so comes as a thief in the night [KJV]." 1 Corinthians 15:52 states, "In a moment, in the twinkling of an eye, at the last trump: for the trumpet shall sound, and the dead shall be raised incorruptible, and we shall be changed [KJV]." The trumpets in this verse may be a direct reference to the blowing of the trumpets during the Feast of Trumpets. There is evidence to suggest that Jesus will return to remove the Church from the tribulation on the Feast of Trumpets. This will then usher in the time of Revelation.

Day of Atonement / Yom Kippur

Leviticus 23:27 states, "On the tenth day of this seventh month there shall be a day of atonement: it shall be a holy convocation unto you; and you shall afflict your souls, and offer an offering made by fire unto the Lord [KJV]." Yom Kippur, or the Day of Atonement, is the holiest day of the Jewish year, and provides prophetic insight into the Second Coming of Jesus the Messiah, the restoration of Israel, and the final judgment of the world. The name alludes to two great atonements: those among the nations who turn to Jesus for cleansing and forgiveness, and Israel for purification during Yom Adonai at the end of days. The Day of Atonement was the only time the High Priest could enter the Holy of Holies and call upon Yahweh to offer blood sacrifice for the sins of the people. This marked the great day of intercession made by the High Priest on behalf of Israel (Leviticus 16).

The Book of Leviticus and the description of the priesthood's duties and responsibilities are foreshadowing of Jesus as the High Priest providing an everlasting atonement with God. Because of this sacrifice, only Jesus is worthy to be the High Priest who can open the scroll described in Revelation 5:2-3,5, which states, "Who is worthy to open the book, and to lose the seals thereof? And no man in heaven, nor in earth, neither under the earth, was able to open the book, neither to look thereon.... And one of the elders saith unto me, 'Weep not: behold, the Lion of the tribe of Judah, the Root of David, hath prevailed to open the book, and to lose the seven seals thereof' [KJV].'"

For the Messianic Jew and Christian, there is a bit of ambivalence about the Day of Atonement. This is due to the two advents of Jesus Christ. He has already been sacrificed on the cross to atone for our sins. Also, the Holy Spirit has already been sent to teach and guide us. However, the covenant between God and the followers of Jesus Christ is not yet ultimately fulfilled since we still await the return of Jesus the Messiah to establish His kingdom on Earth. So, on the one hand we celebrate Yom Kippur because it acknowledges Jesus as our High Priest, but on the other hand, we are saddened because His kingdom on Earth has not yet been established.

Feast of Tabernacles / Sukkot

1 Kings 8 describes how the ark was brought into the temple and dedicated by King Solomon at the beginning of the Feast of Tabernacles. Leviticus 23:34 states, 'The fifteenth day of this seventh month shall be the Feast of Tabernacles for seven days unto the Lord [KJV]." The Feast of Tabernacles or Sukkot is observed in the autumn from Tishri 15 to 21. As described in Exodus 29, Aaron and his descendants of priests are to provide sacrifices in a very specific way. The chapter ends with the following:

"Now this is that which you shall offer upon the altar; two lambs of the first year day by day continually. The one lamb you shall offer in the morning; and the other lamb you shall offer at even: And with the one lamb a tenth deal of flour mingled with the fourth part of a hin (~1 gallon) of beaten oil; and the fourth part of a hin of wine for a drink offering. And the other lamb you shall offer at even, and shall do thereto according to the meat offering of the morning, and according to the drink offering thereof, for a sweet savor, an offering made by fire unto the Lord. This shall be a continual burnt offering throughout your generations at the door of the tabernacle of the congregation before the Lord: where I will meet you, to speak there unto you. And there I will meet with the children of Israel, and the tabernacle shall be sanctified by My glory. And I will sanctify the tabernacle of the congregation, and the altar: I will sanctify also both Aaron and his sons, to minister to Me in the priest's office. And I will dwell among the children of Israel, and will be their God. And they shall know that I am the Lord their God, that brought them forth out of the land of Egypt, that I may dwell among them: I am the Lord their God [Exodus 29:38-46 KJV]."

Much of this last part is written in future tense. It may be a literal description of Israel and animal sacrifices, but it alludes to the sacrifice of Jesus as a permanent and continuous work in our lives to atone for our sins. It also describes the consecrated or dedicated tabernacle where God will live among the children of Israel. This is what the Feast of Tabernacles represents – the establishment of God's kingdom on Earth and the restoration of His people. This is described in more detail in Revelation.

"I saw no temple therein: for the Lord God Almighty and the Lamb are the temple of it. And the city had no need of the sun, neither of the moon, to shine in it: for the glory of God did lighten it, and the

Lamb is the light thereof. And the nations of them which are saved shall walk in the light of it: and the kings of the earth do bring their glory and honor into it [Revelation 21:22-24 KJV]."

There is a relevant point of interest related to the three annual pilgrimage festivals (Feast of Unleavened Bread, Feast of Weeks, and Feast of Tabernacles). First, this represents when God the Father, God the Son, and God the Holy Spirit each came to Earth to fulfill their objectives. God the Son [Jesus] was crucified and resurrected during the Feast of Unleavened Bread. During the Feast of Weeks, God the Holy Spirit [Holy Spirit] came down to Earth to teach and guide us until the church is removed at the rapture. After Satan is removed from the Earth and it is cleansed, God the Father resides with us as described in the Feast of Tabernacles.

From a farming point of view, Unleavened Bread corresponds to the planting season and wheat harvest in the spring, Feast of Weeks corresponds to the barley harvest in the summer, and Feast of Tabernacles corresponds to the fruit harvest in the fall.

From a spiritual point of view, the crucifixion of Jesus was not the end of the story, but merely the beginning. This represents the birth of the church and a New Covenant between God and the followers of Christ. The Pentecost represents the beginning of tremendous growth of the church with the aid of the Holy Spirit. The Sukkot represents the final harvesting of believers through the rapture, tribulation, and eventual restoration of God's chosen people on Earth.

Chapter 5

Bible as History

"A small body of determined spirits fired by an unquenchable faith in their mission can alter the course of history."
- Mahatma Gandhi

Moses lived among the Egyptians. Jesus lived among the Romans. We cannot fully understand their lives without understanding the historical context in which they lived.

What is history? Cicero, a Roman philosopher who lived during the Siege of Jerusalem in 63 BC and the assassination of Julius Caesar in 44 BC, said this about history: "History is the witness that testifies to the passing of time; it illuminates reality, vitalizes memory, provides guidance in daily life, and brings us tidings of antiquity." We study people and events in the past to give us perspective, context, and guidance in the present. The Bible provides perspectives on numerous people and events that extend across 66 books from Genesis to Revelation. Were these people real? Did these events happen?

Archaeology is part of the study of human history and prehistory. It uses a set of guidelines and principles to collect information and explain what that information means. In short, archaeology is about finding the stories behind the physical evidence. It is about putting the pieces of information together into a compelling narrative about the people and events being studied.

As an example of the scientific process, let's look at the objects we see in space. Observers of the past could not touch them. They couldn't just take a spaceship to distant stars and collect samples of their contents. So how do we know that the Earth is not flat, but round? How do we know that the Earth moves around the Sun? We did not know as much in the past as we do know, and that is a clue as to how science works.

Thousands of years ago, some observers took meticulous notes on the positions and movements of many objects we see in the sky, including the Sun, Moon, planets, and stars. They observed patterns in the movements of these objects. The Sun rose in the east and set in the west on a very regular basis. We know this as a Day. They observed that the Moon got brighter and darker in a predictable manner. We know this as a Month. They also observed the cycles in temperatures and positions of the Sun in the sky. We know this as a Year.

Scholars of the past attempted to describe the positional relationships and cycles between the Sun and the Earth based on observations. The geocentric model, which was recorded as early as the 6th Century BC, essentially states that the Sun and stars revolve around the Earth. As observations and studies continued, other scholars tried to apply complex mathematics and modeling to explain the movements of the heavens. 2nd Century AD Greek astronomer Claudius Ptolemaeus (Ptolemy) attempted to codify this model. Ptolemy argued that the Earth was a sphere in the center of the universe. Half the stars were above the horizon and half were below the horizon at any time. These stars were some distance away on a stellar sphere. Similarly, the motions of the Sun, Moon, and planets were explained by a complex series of spheres that moved in relationship to each other. Although the movement of spheres within spheres does explain how the heavens moved, it was cumbersome and difficult to understand.

Although a small few disagreed, this Ptolemaic model remained the standard until the combined efforts of Nicolaus Copernicus (1473-1543 AD), Johannes Kepler (1571-1630 AD), and Galileo Galilei (1564-1642 AD) were able to develop and prove that the Sun was at the center, and that the Earth was the third closest planet to the Sun. They studied. They observed. They spent countless hours gathering information and developing concepts. They were willing to look at and explain the evidence in a new way.

Even though these three were correct, their ideas of a heliocentric universe were not widely accepted. The Catholic Church banned Copernicus' book in 1616 AD and summoned Galileo to an Inquisition in 1633 AD. The influential few with substantial power did what they could to hold back the development of knowledge and science, but in the end, Copernicus, Kepler, and Galileo were vindicated. In the 20th Century, Popes Pius XII and John Paul II made official statements of regret for how the Catholic Church treated Galileo.

This is one of the situations influential scientists want to use to discredit the Church, Christianity, and the Bible. Their fundamental argument is that the Church was so afraid of progress that it abused its power and authority to such a degree that it banned books and threw scientists in jail. It is true that the Roman Catholic Church fought against science, but at the end, there was no need.

True science and being a follower of Christ are not in conflict with each other. In fact, we encourage people to thoroughly research every detail of the Bible. There is a growing number of scientists who are also followers of Christ. Many of them became Christians directly because of their scientific explorations. We encourage people to seek out facts and make conclusions based on facts. Interpretation and consensus are not facts. They are our way to make sense of the information we do have. We fill in missing pieces. Sometimes we get it right. Sometimes we get it wrong. In the cases of both Ptolemy and the Catholic Church, they got it wrong. Science starts with facts. The Bible starts with truth. Bible believing scientists have an advantage over other scientists in that they already know what the final picture looks like.

Our goal is simple: gather facts and create compelling narratives or stories based on the facts provided. We do not feel that the Bible must be proven. We believe the truth of the Bible simply needs to be revealed. Sir Isaac Newton is a well-respected physicist and mathematician. He played a pivotal role in the large-scale acceptance of the works of Copernicus, Kepler, and Galileo. He said this about the Bible, "We account the scriptures of God to be the most sublime philosophy. I find more sure marks of authenticity in the Bible than in any profane history whatsoever."

This book is about the parallels of two people: Moses and Jesus. This chapter is specifically about the historical context in which Moses and Jesus lived. We approach this chapter in three parts. First, we describe the sequence of certain key events in the Bible as related to Moses and Jesus. Second, we link some Biblical people and events with non-Biblical factual records and artifacts. Third, we construct a timeline of actual dates of critical events where the authors feel comfortable that substantial evidence exists. This will provide historical background and context for the people and events surrounding the lives of Jesus and Moses.

Biblical Sequence of Events

In the Beginning (Genesis 1:1, John 1:1)
The Bible states that in the beginning God created the universe.

Abraham Covenant (Genesis 12-17)
God made several promises or covenants with Abraham. First, he will be a blessing. Second, he will have many descendants. Third, his descendants have land set aside for them.

Jacob and Family Moved to Egypt (Genesis 46)
Jacob and all his descendants moved to Goshen, which was located in the eastern delta region of the Nile River. It was located in and around the modern village of Qantir.

Joseph Prepared Egypt for Famine (Genesis 47)
Joseph became Vizier of Egypt, or Pharaoh's highest official. During the seven years of abundance, Joseph ensured that the storehouses were full. When the seven years of famine came, it was so severe that people from surrounding nations came to Egypt for food.

Israelites Crossed the Red Sea (Exodus 14)
Moses and the Israelites crossed the Red Sea through the northern portion of the Gulf of Suez. Pharaoh, 600 chariots, horsemen, thousands of men, gear, and weapons were all swallowed by the sea.

Destruction of Jericho (Joshua 3, 5, 6)
Joshua and the Israelites crossed the Jordan River and celebrated

Passover in the spring. Upon arriving at the walled city of Jericho, they laid siege for six days and destroyed the city on the seventh day.

King Solomon Started to Build the Temple (1 Kings 6)
1 Kings 6:1 states, "It came to pass in the four hundred and eightieth year after the children of Israel were come out of the land of Egypt, in the fourth year of Solomon's reign over Israel, in the month Ziv, which is the second month, that he began to build the house of the Lord [KJV]."

Death of King Solomon (1 Kings 11)
King Solomon was an immensely powerful, wealthy, and influential figure. Shortly after his death, the land of Israel was split into the Northern Kingdom (Samaria) and Southern Kingdom (Judah).

Birth of Jesus Christ (Matthew 1)
Jesus was born during the reign of King Herod, Caesar Augustus, and Governor Quirinius.

Crucifixion of Christ (Matthew 27)
Pontius Pilate was the fifth prefect of the Roman province of Judea. He served under Emperor Tiberius and is best known for the trial and crucifixion of Jesus Christ.

Biblical / Non-Biblical Links & Timeline

The primary purpose of this section is to provide connections between the Bible and science. We want to place some people and events within the Bible into a larger context by also looking at historical and scientific evidence. Each connection is a pylon of understanding that becomes part of your foundation of faith. Faith is not blind, and it is not for the uncommitted. It requires fervent prayer and consistent communication with God. It requires academic study, and it requires humble service.

The people selected are major characters within the Bible. The events selected are short term and are corroborated by external historical and scientific evidence. They demonstrate the accuracy of the Bible, which ultimately places the lives of Moses and Jesus into a larger context.

Do we know more about events that occurred one year ago or a thousand years ago? The obvious answer is that generally the more recent an event is, the more we know about it. Using this as a guideline, we would like to create a chronology and discussion moving backwards in time.

Biblical people and events discussed in more detail include:
- Jesus (Matthew, Mark, Luke, John)
- 70 Weeks of Daniel (Daniel 9)
- Construction of King Solomon's Temple (1 Kings 6)
- Judge Deborah (Judges 4-5)
- Battle of Jericho (Joshua 2-6)
- Joshua (Exodus, Numbers, Deuteronomy, Joshua)
- Moses (Exodus, Leviticus, Numbers, Deuteronomy)
- Joseph (Genesis 30-50)
- Abraham (Genesis 11-25)
- Nimrod and the Tower of Babel (Genesis 10-11)

Empires, dynasties, and civilizations discussed in more detail include:
- Julio-Claudian Dynasty (Luke, Acts, Philippians)

- Herodian Dynasty (Matthew, Mark, Luke, John, Acts)
- Hasmonean Dynasty (Daniel, Zechariah, 1 & 2 Maccabees)
- Medo-Persian / Achaemenid Empire (Ezra, Nehemiah, Esther, Daniel, Haggai, Zechariah, Malachi)
- Divided Kingdom (1 Kings, 2 Kings, 2 Chronicles, Isaiah, Jeremiah, Lamentations, Ezekiel, Hosea, Joel, Amos, Obadiah, Jonah, Micah, Nahum, Habakkuk, Zephaniah)
- Assyria (Genesis, 2 Kings, 1 & 2 Chronicles, Ezra, Nehemiah, Psalms, Isaiah, Jeremiah, Lamentations, Ezekiel, Hosea, Micah, Nahum, Zephaniah, Zechariah)
- Babylon (Joshua, 2 Kings, 1 & 2 Chronicles, Ezra, Nehemiah, Esther, Psalms, Isaiah, Jeremiah, Ekekiel, Daniel, Micah, Zechariah, Matthew, Acts, 1 Peter, Revelation)
- Egypt (Genesis, Exodus, Leviticus, Numbers, Deuteronomy, Joshua, Judges, 1 & 2 Samuel, 1 & 2 Kings, 1 & 2 Chronicles, Ezra, Nehemiah, Psalms, Proverbs, Isaiah, Jeremiah, Lamentations, Ezekiel, Daniel, Hosea, Joel, Amos, Micah, Nahum, Haggai, Zechariah, Matthew, Acts, Hebrews, Jude, Revelation)
- Sumer (Genesis)

Julio-Claudian Dynasty

There were 3 primary historians who wrote down information around the time of Julio-Claudian Dynasty:

Suetonius (~69-122 AD) was a Roman of the equestrian order (lower of the 2 aristocratic classes). His most important surviving work is a set of biographies of 12 Roman rulers from Julius Caesar (49-44 BC) to Domitian (81-96 AD) entitled De Vita Caesarum.

Tacitus (~56-120 AD) was a Roman senator who examined the

reigns from Tiberius (14-37 AD) to the early reign of Vespasian (69-79 AD) in 2 major works - Annals and Histories.

Josephus (37-100 AD) was a Romano-Jewish historian. He fought against the Romans in 1st Jewish-Roman War (67 AD). He later became a friend of Titus, the son of Emperor Vespasian (69-79 AD). He wrote The Jewish War (~75 AD) and Antiquities of the Jews (~94 AD).

Dynastic succession was more through adoption than direct descendant. The sitting ruler chose the next in line.

Julius Caesar (October 49 BC – March 15, 44 BC): Successful general and last leader of the Roman Republic. He was assassinated by Roman Senator Marcus Junius Brutus and other Roman officials.

Augustus (January 16, 27 BC – August 19, 14 AD): Great-nephew and adopted son of Julius Caesar. He was the 1st Emperor of Rome. He is mentioned in Luke 2:1.

Tiberius (September 18, 14 AD – March 16, 37 AD): Step-son and adopted son of Augustus. Tiberius was the step-son of Augustus, grand-uncle of Caligula, paternal uncle of Claudius, and great-grand uncle of Nero. Tiberius was one of Rome's greatest generals. He is mentioned in Luke 3:1.

Caligula (March 18, 37 AD – January 24, 41 AD): Great-nephew and adoptive grandson of Tiberius. Although he is described as a noble and moderate ruler during the first six months of his reign, he was described as an insane tyrant for the remainder of his reign. He worked to increase the unconstrained personal power of the emperor. He was assassinated by officers of the Praetorian Guard and Roman senators.

Claudius (January 25, 41 AD – October 13, 54 AD): Uncle of Caligula. Nephew of Tiberius. He was an able and efficient administrator. He was also an ambitious builder, constructing many new roads, aqueducts, and canals across the Roman Empire. During his reign the Roman Empire began the conquest of Britain. He is mentioned in Acts 11:28 and Acts 18:2.

Nero (October 13, 54 AD – June 9, 68 AD): Great-great-grandson of Augustus. During his reign, General Corbulo conducted a successful war and negotiated peace with the Parthian Empire. General Suetonius Paulinus crushed a major revolt in Britain led by the Iceni Queen Boudica. The Bosporan Kingdom was briefly annexed to the empire, and the First Jewish–Roman War began. Although not mentioned by name, he is most likely referred to in Acts 25 and Philippians 4:22.

<u>Jesus and the Census</u> (Luke 2, Matthew 2)

There was a decree for a census during the times of Caesar Augustus and Quirinius Governor of Syria. Herod was King of Judea. Also, John the Baptist began his ministry in the fifteenth year of the reign of Tiberius Caesar. Pontius Pilate was governor of Judea, Herod was tetrarch of Galilee, Philip was tetrarch of Iturea & Trachonitis, Lysanias was tetrarch of Abilene, and Annas & Caiaphas were high priests. Jesus was born, lived, and died during the reigns of Caesar Augustus and his step-son Caesar Tiberius. Caesar Augustus, also known as Gaius Octavius, is the grandnephew and adopted son of Julius Caesar.

Crucifixion of Christ / Birth of Jesus Christ

According to consensus, King Herod the Great died in 4 BC and Publius Sulpicius Quirinius held the first census in 6 AD. These dates contradict details in the Bible concerning the birth of Jesus. How can one hold a census during the reign of a king who's been dead for a decade? The accepted death of Herod the Great as 4 BC is also a major reason for placing the birth of Jesus in 6 BC.

If we take a closer look at historical evidence, these apparent contradictions fade away. First, let's look at the date of the crucifixion of Jesus. A critical piece of information is in Luke 3:1 as related to the 15th year of the reign of Tiberius Caesar. According to most scholars, he began his reign on September 18 (~Tishri 6), 14 AD, when the Roman Senate officially confirmed him as the second Emperor of the Roman Empire. This is a critical piece of information. Many of the other dates provided are derived from the date in which Caesar Tiberius began his reign. His father was Caesar Augustus who was considered the first emperor of Rome. He reigned for 40 years, and died on August 19, 14 AD. The great uncle of Augustus was Julius Caesar who died on March 15, 44 BC. Because of the existence of multiple historical records related to the activities of Rome's leaders, the date Tiberius gained power can be considered reasonably accurate.

John the Baptist began his work sometime between September 29 AD and September 30 AD – which represents the 15th year of Tiberius (Luke 3:1). Jesus was about 30 years old (between 29 and 31 years old) when He began His ministry (Luke 3:23) which encompassed three Passovers (John 2:13, John 6:4, John 12:1). According to Matthew 4, Jesus was tempted for 40 days directly after His baptism. Afterwards He gathered His disciples and started to perform miracles in Galilee all before the first Passover of His ministry. Giving about 60 days for all this, we can conclude that John the Baptist started his ministry somewhere between September 29 AD and February 30 AD.

The Passover mentioned in John 2:13 would be Nisan 14, 30 AD (~April 5, 30 AD). Jesus was crucified two years later on Nisan 14, 32 AD (~April 14, 32 AD). The youngest Jesus could be at the time of crucifixion is a little more than 29+2 years or 31 years old. The oldest He could be at the time of crucifixion is a little less than 31+3 years or 34 years old. Working backward, the birth of Jesus was between 1 AD and 3 BC.

Two chronological conflicts must be reconciled to find the birth date of Jesus and to demonstrate that the Bible was actually correct in the information it provided: date of death of King Herod and census of Quirinius. The primary reason scholars state that Herod died in 4 BC is because the historian Josephus associated his death with a lunar eclipse, which is commonly associated with the one on March 13, 4 BC. There were, however, several other eclipses during that period: September 15, 5 BC, January 10, 1 BC, and December 29, 1 BC. Matthew 2:16 states that Herod killed all male children around Bethlehem that were under two years of age. It would be a safe assumption that Jesus would have been under two years old at the time of the proclamation. Without getting into a complicated discussion as to which eclipse is associated with Herod's death, some scholars argue for a 4 BC eclipse, and others argue for a 1 BC eclipse. Based on this, Herod could have died in 1 BC, and Jesus could have been born somewhere between 1 BC and 3 BC. We will come back to this discussion later in this chapter.

That brings us to Publius Sulpicius Quirinius. Records show that he ruled over Syria from 6-9 AD. This makes the first census in 6 AD. There are records, however, that show that this was his second tenure in power and not his first. A fragment of marble was discovered in 1764 AD near Tibur / Tivoli with an inscription. This artifact is preserved in the Lateran Museum of Christian Antiquities in Rome. The inscription records the career and honors of a Roman official who lived in the reign of Augustus, and survived that emperor. He conquered a nation. He was rewarded with Roman honors. He governed Asia as proconsul, and he twice governed Syria as legatus of the divine Augustus. This artifact demonstrates that Quirinius may have been governor of Syria twice. The second time was 6-9 AD. Scholars who have studied this in detail place the first governorship of Syria as early as 5 BC and as late as 1 BC. Now that the facts have been reviewed, Herod died in 1 BC, and Quirinius ruled Syria somewhere between 5 BC and 1 BC. Data points to the birth date of Jesus between 3 BC and 1 BC.

It is possible to get a more exact date for the birth of Jesus. To narrow this range, let's look at John the Baptist. Zacharias, the father of John the Baptist, was a priest of the Abijah division (Luke 1:5). Elizabeth was six months pregnant with John when Mary became pregnant with Jesus (Luke 1:26). 1 Chronicles 24 established 24 priestly divisions in which Abijah was eighth in rotation to serve at the temple. We cannot be absolutely certain that the priestly rotation sequence described in 1 Chronicles 24 was still in effect at the time of Jesus. The destruction of the temple and exile in Babylon disrupted this cycle. If we assume for a moment that priestly duties started rotation on Nisan 1 and lasted for two weeks, the conception of John would have occurred 15 to 16 weeks later in mid-summer. This would place his birth about nine months later in the spring, possibly on or near Passover. Six months later would place the birth of Jesus in the fall, possibly during the Feast of Trumpets (see Chapter 4). Feasts have importance in God's timetable. Jesus was crucified on Passover and resurrected on the Feast of Firstfruits. Also, the Holy Spirit descended during the Feast of Weeks. There is a strong case that Jesus was born on the Feast of Trumpets. This would then place Jesus' birthday on Tishri 1 (~September 29), 2 BC, or Tishri 1 (~September 11), 3 BC. A birth date of September 1 BC does not reconcile as well with the evidence available. We think the most likely of the three options is Tishri 1, 2 BC.

One more important date to toss in is related to the rebuilding of Jerusalem after the Babylonian exile in 586 BC. King Solomon built the first temple (which is discussed later in this chapter). Zerubbabel and Ezra built the second temple (Ezra 3:8, Zechariah 4:9) which was dedicated on March 12, 515 BC. According to Josephus, Herod began to rebuild the temple in the 18th year of his reign. Also, Herod the Great ruled for about 37 years. Most scholars place the beginning of his reign when he overthrew the Hasmoneans in 37 BC. This is consistent with having his death in 1 BC. The 18th year of his reign would be ~19 BC. John 2:20 contains an interesting phrase: "It has taken forty-six years to build this temple..." One suggestion is that the temple has been under reconstruction for 46 years at the time this situation occurred. If the 46 years relates to the time of reconstruction, 46 years after 19 BC is 27 AD. This does not match our date of 30 AD for dating John 2:13-20 and the cleansing of the temple. Upon closer look, Josephus dated the proclamation to rebuild the temple to Herod's 18th year. It would have taken time to obtain materials, designs, and labor to begin the project. Actual construction would have begun some time later, perhaps ~16-17 BC. In this context, John 2:20 makes more sense. The temple was still under construction 46 years after actual reconstruction began. So, the proclamation to rebuild was made ~19 BC. Reconstruction began ~17 BC. History tells us that Herod's temple was finally finished in 64 AD – which is a year of Jubilee (discussed later in this chapter).

Greece, Hasmonean Dynasty, and Herodian Dynasty

Alexander the Great (Daniel 7, 8, 11, 1 Maccabees 1:1) succeeded his father Philip II to the throne of Macedon at the age of twenty. He spent most of his ruling years on an unprecedented military campaign through Europe, Asia, and Africa. He developed one of the largest empires of the ancient world by the age of thirty, stretching from Greece and Egypt in the west to portions of India in the east. He is widely considered one of history's most successful military commanders.

After he was poisoned in 323 BC, his empire was divided into 4 power centers: Ptolemaic (Egypt), Seleucid (Mesopotamia, and Central Asia), Attalid (Anatolia / Turkey), and Antigonid (Macedon / Greece). The Seleucid Dynasty (312-63 BC) was founded by Seleucus I Nicator upon the breakup of Alexander the Great's conquests, and it existed until it was overthrown by Roman General Pompey.

The Hasmonean Dynasty was established by Simon Maccabaeus about two decades after his brother Judah the Maccabee defeated the Seleucid army during the Maccabean Revolt (167-160 BC). Events during this time period are described in the Apocryphal books 1 Maccabees and 2 Maccabees. They are also described in the first book of The Jewish War by Jewish historian Flavius Josephus.

Seleucid leader Antiochus IV Epiphanes sacked Jerusalem and its Temple, suppressing Jewish and Samaritan religious and cultural observances. He imposed Hellenistic cultural and religious practices. The local Jewish population in Jerusalem revolted and fought back. As a result of this Maccabean Revolt, the Maccabees gained local control of Israel. Due to a weak Seleucid empire, the Hasmoneans ruled Israel independently from 110-63 BC.

Rome took control of the region in 63 BC. General Pompey successfully captured Jerusalem. Hasmonean rule was replaced by the installation of King Herod the Great in 37 BC. According to Josephus, Herod the Great ruled for 37 years, which would place his death in 1 BC. Herod Antipas (1 BC-39 AD) succeeded Herod the Great. He is the Herod mentioned in the Gospels during the ministry and crucifixion of Jesus Christ. Herod Agrippa (41-44 AD) was the last ruler with the royal title of the Herodian Dynasty. He was a close friend of Roman Emperor Caligula. He is the Herod mentioned in Acts 12:1 He killed James the son of Zebedee and imprisoned Peter. He was placed in charge of parts of the territory of Syria and Jordan by Roman Emperor Caligula. He was placed in charge of Israel by Roman Emperor Claudius.

70 Weeks of Daniel and the Dead Sea Scrolls

Daniel 9:20-27 has been called the Seventy Weeks of Daniel prophecy. It is one of the most powerful prophecies in the entire Bible based on both its detail and its accuracy. It was written by Daniel during the Hebrew exile in Babylon that started when King Nebuchadnezzar II besieged Judah during the third year of the reign of King Jehoiakim (Daniel 1:1), which corresponds to 586 BC. Many non-believing scholars state that it was written around the second century BC because of its style, composition, and content. Yet the captivity of Israel described within the book took place primarily during the sixth century BC.

Frank M. Cross, a professor of Asian languages at Harvard University, studied the Dead Sea Scrolls of Qumran discovered in 1947 AD. He was part of the early team of editors appointed in 1953. In the second edition of his book - The Ancient Library of Qumran – he wrote: "One copy of Daniel is inscribed in the script of the late second century BC; in some ways it is more striking than that of the oldest manuscripts from Qumran." This convinced many modern scholars that Daniel was written much later than the 6th Century BC. They want to date it to the time in which the Septuagint was being finalized in the late 2nd Century BC (see Chapter 1).

A critical question to ask is how accurate our current version of Daniel is, and when was it written? The Dead Sea Scrolls provide some details on this. At least 8 scrolls of the Book of Daniel have been found in Qumran. The translated and published material found near the Dead Sea has offered some valuable data. Four conclusions can be made about these 8 Dead Sea scrolls of Daniel:

1) The 8 scrolls are essentially in agreement with each other.
2) Although there are some rare minor variations that agree with the Septuagint Greek version, the clear majority of material is in alignment with the agreed upon version of the Masoretic Hebrew text.
3) None of the fragments contain any of the additions found in the Greek manuscripts of Daniel, such as the Prayer of Azariah, the Song of the Three Young Men, and the Story of Susanna.

4) The change from Hebrew to Aramaic in Daniel 2:4 and Aramaic to Hebrew in Daniel 8:1 are preserved in the Dead Sea Scrolls and are in agreement with the Masoretic Text.

Based on the overwhelming conformity of the Qumran Daniel scrolls with each other and with the Masoretic Text, the Hebrew/Aramaic Masoretic text version of the Book of Daniel is the most accurate and best-preserved version. Also, because of this strong agreement, and because these scrolls were discovered with other widely accepted canonical books of the Bible, such as Deuteronomy, Kings, Psalms, and Isaiah, the Book of Daniel was considered important and canonical. It was preserved and protected by Hebrew scribes. Aramaic was the common language during the Babylonian exile, whereas Greek was the common language during the time of the Maccabeans. Based on evidence, it is more likely that Daniel was written during the exile in Babylon in the 6th Century BC than during the Maccabean revolt in the 160s BC against the Greek Seleucid dynasty. Therefore, the Book of Daniel predates the Greek translation of the Bible.

Daniel 9 contains one of the most detailed and accurate prophecies in the Bible. So what is it about the chapter that some scholars want to deny? The following are verses 24-27:

"Seventy weeks are determined upon your people and upon your holy city, to finish the transgression, and to make an end of sins, and to make reconciliation for iniquity, and to bring in everlasting righteousness, and to seal up the vision and prophecy, and to anoint the most Holy.

Know therefore and understand, that from the going forth of the commandment to restore and to build Jerusalem unto the Messiah the Prince shall be seven weeks, and threescore and two weeks: the street shall be built again, and the wall, even in troublous times.

And after threescore and two weeks shall Messiah be cut off, but not for Himself: and the people of the prince that shall come shall destroy the city and the sanctuary; and the end thereof shall be with a flood, and unto the end of the war desolations are determined.

And he shall confirm the covenant with many for one week: and in the midst of the week he shall cause the sacrifice and the oblation to cease, and for the overspreading of abominations he shall make it desolate, even until the consummation, and that determined shall be poured upon the desolate [KJV]."

As stated previously in chapter 4, one prophetic year is 360 days. This prophecy in Daniel 9 is about Jesus Christ and His work on Earth and contains three parts:
1) 7 Weeks of Years = 49 Hebrew Years = 17,640 Days
2) 62 Weeks of Years = 434 Hebrew Years = 156,240 Days
3) 1 Week of Years = 7 Hebrew Years = 2,520 Days

The prophetic time clock described in this chapter began at the command to restore and rebuild Jerusalem. History records that the Medo-Persian (Achaemenid) emperor Artaxerxes issued such a decree on March 14, 445 BC. The rebuilding of Jerusalem is described in the Book of Nehemiah. Efforts to rebuild began in the spring of 445 BC and finished in late autumn of 396 BC – exactly 49 years or 17,640 days.

There were two times when Jesus entered the city of Jerusalem. The first was when He cleansed the temple as described in John 2. The second was during His triumphal entry as described in Matthew 21. The Daniel 9 prophecy describes this second event, which occurred on Nisan 10 or April 6, 32 AD.

How many days are there between March 14, 445 BC and April 6, 32 AD? If you deduct one year between 1 BC and 1 AD, we calculate 476 years, 24 days or 173,764 days. However, we must add 119 days to account for leap years (476/4=119). We now have 173,883 days. So, what about the difference of three days? There is a slight inaccuracy in the Julian calendar when compared to the solar year. The Royal Observatory in London calculates that a Julian year is 1/128th of a day longer than the Jewish year. When we divide 476 by 128, we get three days. Subtracting three from our figure above, we arrive at exactly 173,880 days. There were exactly 17,640 days between the decree to rebuild Jerusalem and its completion. There were exactly 173,880 days between this decree and the triumphant entry of Jesus into Jerusalem.

There is more. Jesus was crucified on the Passover of 32 AD. This is consistent with our determination in chapter 5. The best interpretation of the data is that the triumphal entry of Jesus occurred on Nisan 10, 32 AD. His crucifixion occurred on Nisan 14, 32 AD. There is some discrepancy, however, converting between the Hebrew Lunar calendar and the Roman Solar calendar. The amount of time between Nisan 10 and Nisan 14 is not the same as between April 6 (Triumphal Entry) and April 14 (our date for Passover) as provided within the chapters of this book. This difference is caused by a few things. First, a specific date starts in the morning in the Roman calendar system. However, a specific date starts in the evening in the Hebrew calendar system. Second, the

Roman calendar is based on movements of the Sun, whereas the Hebrew calendar is based on movements of the Moon. Third, there are 365.242 days in a year – not 365.25. This discrepancy throws the calendars off one day every 128 years.

Some interpretations of these calendar systems place Passover on the morning of April 14. Other interpretations place Passover on the evening of April 9. The actual conversion from the Jewish lunar calendar to the Roman solar calendar requires some moderately complicated mathematical calculations. At the end of the day, important things to remember about this is that God's message to Daniel was thorough and accurate, that the triumphal entry occurred on Nisan 10, 32 AD, and that the crucifixion occurred on Nisan 14, 32 AD.

After the crucifixion of Jesus Christ, Israel as a nation was destroyed and its people dispersed. Following the death and resurrection of Jesus, relations between the Jews and the Roman Empire steadily worsened until the Jews rebelled in 66 AD. The Romans were overpowered at first and withdrew troops from the region. After Roman general Titus Flavius Vespasianus (aka Vespasian) made himself emperor in 69 AD, a Roman army under the leadership of his son Titus reached Jerusalem in 70 AD. After a siege of about three months, the people of Jerusalem were greatly weakened by food shortages. The Romans successfully stormed the Temple and the lower city. Both were destroyed rapidly by uncontrolled fires throughout the city. Roman legions poured into the city and easily destroyed any opposition. They tore down every building except three towers and the western wall, which Titus left as monuments to his victory. In all, over one million Jews were killed. For those who survived, many left the region and settled in other areas around the world.

The last week of Daniel is described in more detail in the Book of Revelation. Chapter 6 describes some of these events in more detail. It is related to the second coming of Jesus, the reestablishment of the nation of Israel, and the establishment of His kingdom on Earth. Revelation describes this time frame as 7 years. Most of the trials, tribulations, and judgments which Revelation is famous for occur in the second half of this 7-year time period. The detail and accuracy of the Daniel 9 prophecy is undeniable. This is exactly why non-believing scholars want to discredit it.

Divided Kingdom

When King Solomon died in 931 BC, Israel split into two kingdoms: Israel and Judah. The kingdom of Israel comprised the territories of the tribes of Asher, Dan, Ephraim, Gad, Issachar, Manasseh, Naphtali, Reuben, Simeon, and Zebulun. Its capital was Samaria. The kingdom of Judah comprised the territories of the tribes of Benjamin and Judah. Its capital was Jerusalem. The northern tribes refused to accept Rehoboam, son of Solomon, as the rightful heir to the throne. They installed Jeroboam as their king who was from the tribe of Ephraim. Rehoboam became the king of Judah.

The Bible relates many stories of interactions with the Assyrians and the Babylonians. These cross-references form a framework that have been useful in dating many key events that took place after the death of King Solomon in 931 BC and before the fall of the Neo-Babylonian Empire by the Medo-Persians in 539 BC. Refer to the

Promise Keeper

Appendix for dates related to the kings of Israel, Judah, Assyria, and Babylon.

At the height of its power, the Neo-Assyrian Empire (911-612 BC) spoke Aramaic and Akkadian and controlled lands from the Persian Gulf in the east to Turkey in the north to Egypt in the west. Its capital was Ninevah. Five Assyrian kings are mentioned in the Bible: Tiglath-pileser III, Shalmaneser V, Sargon II, Sennacherib, and Esarhaddon.

Menahem, king of Israel, gave Tiglath-pileser III 1000 talents of silver while Azariah / Uzziah was king of Judah (2 Kings 15:17-22, 1 Chronicles 5:26). Shalmaneser V made Israel a vassal or subordinate of the Assyrian Empire while Hoshea was king of Israel and Ahaz was king of Judah (2 Kings 17:1-4).

The King of Assyria besieged Samaria for 3 years. This is mentioned in 2 Kings 17:1-6. Although the Bible does not mention it directly, archaeologists have uncovered some interesting information related to this 3 year siege. The siege was started by Shalmaneser V. However, he was overthrown by his younger brother Sargon II in 722 BC. In that same year, Sargon II conquered the Northern Kingdom of Israel, which represents the 9th year of the reign of Hoshea king of Israel. This means that verses 1-4 refer to Shalmaneser V, and verses 5-6 refer to Sargon II.

In 612 BC, the Medes, Persians, Scythians, Cimmerians, and Chaldeans (under Nabopolassar) formed an alliance to destroy Ninevah and the Assyrian Empire. Nabopolassar is father of Nebuchadnezzar II. The Chaldeans originated from the northwest side of the Persian Gulf, which is the same region that Abraham was born (Genesis 11:27-31). The Chaldeans were absorbed into the Babylonian Empire and ruled it from 626-539 BC. Four Babylonian kings are mentioned in the Bible: Nebuchadnezzar II (605-562 BC), Merodach / Amel-Marduk (562-560 BC), Nergal-Sharezer / Neriglissar (560-556 BC), and Belshazzar (550-539 BC). Nebuchadnezzar II besieged Jerusalem. Jehoiachin, king of Judah, was taken prisoner in the eighth year of his reign in 586 BC (2 Kings 24:8-12). This is corroborated by the Babylonian Chronicles, which are tablets that recorded various historical events in Babylonian history. Nebuchadnezzar II (Nabu-kudurri-usur II) is associated with the Hanging Gardens of Babylon. Merodach (Amel-Marduk) released Jehoiachin from prison in the 37th year of captivity (2 Kings 25:27). Belshazzar was co-regent of Babylon after his father, King Nabonidus, went into exile in 550 BC. He is mentioned in Daniel 5 and was slain when the Medo-Persians gained control of Babylon in 539 BC.

Some kings of Israel and Judah are reported in Assyrian and Babylonian records. These include: Ahab, Jehu, Omri, Jehoash, Manasseh, Jehoiachin, and Zedekiah. The Monolith Inscription of Shalmaneser III records the king's first six military campaigns against the Arameans in Syria. The campaign of year six, 853 BC, mentions Ahab, king of Israel, as being part of an anti-Assyrian coalition that confronted the Assyrians at Qarqar on the Orontes River in western Syria. The Black Obelisk of Shalmaneser III records another military campaign in 841 BC. He defeated Damascus and turned south to Israel. He received tribute from Tyre, Sidon, and Jehu, son of Omri. The Stela of Adad-Nirari III (~790 BC) mentions tribute from Jehoash king of Israel. Manasseh, king of Judah, was mentioned in manuscripts by two Assyrian kings: Esarhaddon and Ashurbanipal.

Promise Keeper

The Babylonian Chronicle records the removal of Jehoiachin as king of Judah and replacement of Zedekiah as king.

Brief History of Egypt

Egypt was a major political, economic, and military power throughout a significant part of the Old Testament. Therefore, it would be helpful to have a basic understanding of Egyptian history. Egyptian chronology is broken down into 9 primary dynastic or family groups.
** Note: D = Dynasty

Predynastic Period (D0-2): There is limited information.

Old Kingdom (D3-6): Khufu, Djedefre, and Kafre of the 4th dynasty built the Great Pyramids of Giza and the Sphinx.

1st Intermediate Period (D7-10): There is limited information. It was a time of chaos.

Middle Kingdom (D11-12): Opened regional trade with other nations. It was the time of Senuret I, II, III and Amenemhat I, II, III, IV.

2nd Intermediate Period (D13-17): The Hyksos invaded (1400s BC) and ruled Egypt for a period of time. There is limited information.

New Kingdom (D18-20): It was a time of military dominance and great building projects. Pharaohs include: Amenhotep, Tutankhamun, and Ramesses.

3rd Intermediate Period (D21-25): Collapse of the Egyptian Empire at the end of the Bronze Age (~1200 BC).

Late Period (D26-31): There was a mix of Egyptian and Persian rulers.

Hellenistic Period: Greek rule by Alexander the Great (332-323 BC) and the Ptolemy Dynasty. The last pharaoh was Cleopatra VII Philopator who was assassinated on August 12, 30 BC.

<u>King Solomon Started to Build the Temple / Israelites Crossed the Red Sea</u>

Numerous major events occurred between the time the Israelites crossed the Red Sea forty years after the Exodus from Egypt and construction of King Solomon's Temple four years into his reign. This entire time span, according to the Holy Bible, is 480 years (1 Kings 6:1). These events, in chronological order, include: exodus from Egypt, crossing the Red Sea, crossing the Jordan River, Battle of Jericho, judgeship of Deborah, and construction of King Solomon's Temple. Some of these events will be discussed separately, and out of chronological order. This is designed to provide the best method for the most understanding.

Battle of Jericho:

According to Joshua 3-6, the Israelites crossed the Jordan River. They celebrated the Passover, which would be Nisan 14. They ate some of the fresh grain of the land. Three days later, on Nisan 17, the manna that had sustained them for forty years stopped.

After the celebration, the Israelites marched around the city of Jericho for seven days. On the seventh day, after their seventh circuit around the city, the priests blew their trumpets, the people shouted, and the walls of the city fell. They then killed every living thing within the city and burned it. Only Rahab, who had hidden the Israelite spies, and her family were spared from the destruction.

In the 19th and 20th centuries, several organized excavations were performed on the remains of Jericho. The most notable were those of the British archaeologists John Garstang (1930–1936) and Kathleen Kenyon (1952–1958). Garstang found fallen city walls, burned stores of grain and evidence of destruction of the city by fire, which is in line with the narrative provided in the Book of Joshua. Garstang asked Kenyon to review pottery found. Kathleen Kenyon found much of the same evidence - collapsed walls, stores of grain and an ash layer from a massive fire. However, she reached a completely different conclusion based on her review of the pottery. Rather than supporting the Biblical account, she denied it stating that it happened at the wrong time. She dated the material about 150 years earlier than Garstang did. Her statements had a major impact on the scholarly world. Many hailed her findings as proof that the Bible was historically unreliable and that it could not be trusted. Detailed reports on her findings at Jericho weren't published until several years after her death.

Archaeologist Bryant Wood - then a visiting professor at the University of Toronto - examined her findings. He realized she had based her dating on the fact that she did not find a kind of imported pottery found at other sites in the Near East - thus Jericho must have been unoccupied at the time. The problem, Dr. Wood learned, was that she had excavated a poor section of town in which the inhabitants could not have afforded to buy and use such imported pottery. He also discovered that Kathleen Kenyon had found indigenous pottery that dates precisely to the time of the Biblical conquest of the city, but ignored it. She also overlooked the fact that her predecessor, John Garstang, found painted pottery from the time of the conquest. Egyptian amulets he found at a nearby cemetery also indicated the site was regularly inhabited for several centuries up until the city's fall. Thus, there was no occupation gap as she had supposed. The unusually large stores of carbonized grain found in the ruins showed that the city had endured only a short siege, which the Bible numbers at seven days. The grain had been recently harvested, which points to a springtime assault. Also, because grain was a valuable commodity almost always plundered by conquering forces, the large amount of grain left in the ruins is unusual - but consistent with the Bible. The destruction was nearly complete. Walls and floors were blackened by fire, and every room was filled with fallen bricks, timbers, and household utensils. The evidence is consistent with the story told in the Book of Joshua.

King Solomon reigned 970-931 BC. Construction of the temple was four years into his reign which would be 966 BC. According to the Bible, the Exodus occurred 480 years earlier or 1446 BC. The Israelites crossed the Jordan River and entered Canaan forty years after the Exodus or 1406 BC. This is discussed in more detail below. Many Jewish scholars date the 7th day of conquest where the walls fell on Nisan 28 or around May 14, 1406 BC. This means they would have started the week long siege the day after the Feast of Unleavened Bread ended. Archaeologist Bryant Wood dated the fall of Jericho at around 1400 BC, which is evidence that corroborates the Bible narrative. The Passover associated with the crossing of the Jordan River prior to the conquest of Jericho was on Nisan 14, 1406

BC, or around April 30, 1406 BC (Joshua 5:10).

Ramesses II and the Judges of Israel:

Genesis 47:11, Exodus 1:11, Exodus 12:37, Numbers 33:3, and Numbers 33:5 mention either a city or a land called Raamses or Rameses. This has led to the Ramesses Exodus Theory which states that Ramesses II was the pharaoh of the Exodus. According to many Egyptologists, Ramesses II was born circa 1303 BC and reigned from 1279–1213 BC. We are in general agreement with these dates. He was the third pharaoh of the Nineteenth Dynasty of Egypt and part of the New Kingdom. He led military expeditions northeast into Western Asia and south into Nubia (modern day Sudan), generating central control over a significant amount of real estate. Ramesses II was a prolific builder. He covered the land from the Delta to Nubia (Sudan) with buildings in a way no leader before him had done. He also founded a new capital city in the Delta during his reign called Pi-Ramesses. It is believed that he used large numbers of slaves to construct them.

If Ramesses II is the pharaoh of the Exodus, this creates numerous problems for the chronology of events in the Bible. Let's assume for a moment that the crossing of the Red Sea occurred at the end of his reign in 1213 BC. The Battle of Jericho would have had to occur in 1173 BC (40 years later). This would mean that all the events between the conquest of Jericho, through the lives of King Saul and King David, to the end of the reign of Solomon would have had to occur in about 242 years. The Bible describes this interval as approximately 475 years. Another element to throw into this discussion is that there is no evidence of a Jewish presence in Egypt during the time of Ramesses II. Many Egyptologists would use this as proof that the story of Exodus as described in the Bible is wrong and cannot be trusted.

Another option is that the Exodus had already occurred prior to the time of Ramesses II, and that the mention of Rameses in the Bible was about some person or geographic region that predated the 13th Century BC. The Merneptah Stele was written by the son and successor of Ramesses II, Pharaoh Merneptah. He was the fourth ruler of the Nineteenth Dynasty of Egypt. According to Egyptologists, he ruled Egypt for almost ten years between summer 1213 and May 2, 1203 BC. He was the thirteenth son of Ramesses II and only came to power because all his older brothers had died. By the time he ascended to the throne he was almost sixty years old. The Merneptah Stele references Israel as an existing foreign nation.

The Amarna Letters are also consistent with the Exodus occurring during the end of the Middle Kingdom of Egypt. The Amarna Letters are 382 clay tablets written in the regional language of diplomacy – Akkadian. They are correspondence letters between heads of states and regional leaders. 14 are from Babylon. 2 are from Assyria. 14 are from Mitanni. 2 are from Arzawa. 8 are from Alashiya. 4 are from Hatti. 23 are from Syria. 160 are from Lebanon. The remainder - over 150 – are from Canaan. This archive contains a wealth of information about cultures, kingdoms, events, and individuals from a period in which few written records still exist. Some of the leaders mentioned in these letters include: Pharaoh Amenhotep III, Pharaoh Akhenaten, King of Babylon Kadashman-Enlil I, Tushratta of Mitanni, Lib'ayu of Shechem, Abdi-Heba of Jerusalem, and King Rib-Hadda of Byblos.

Amenhotep III and Akhenaten are from the Eighteenth Dynasty of

Egypt and therefore pre-date Ramesses II. The archive spans between 15 and 30 years. It dates between the last decade of the reign of Amenhotep III to the second year of the reign of Tutankhamen. This is when the city of Amarna was abandoned and the capital was moved to Thebes. Although definitive dates are still being discussed, some Egyptologists date this archive from about 1350's to 1332 BC. The archive mentions a group of people called the Habiru. This was the name given by various Egyptian, Akkadian, Hittite, Mitanni, and Ugaritic sources to a group of people living as nomadic invaders in areas of the Fertile Crescent from Northeastern Mesopotamia and Iran to the borders of Egypt in Canaan. Depending on the source and time, these Habiru are variously described as nomadic or semi-nomadic, rebels, outlaws, raiders, mercenaries, bowmen, servants, slaves, and migrant laborers. The Habiru are often identified as Hebrews by scholars. If all this is true, this is more evidence that would place the Israelites in the region of Canaan in the 1300's BC, which again is consistent with the Bible, and inconsistent with Ramesses II being the pharaoh of the Exodus.

The Amarna Letters would have been during the time sequence described in the Book of Judges. More specifically, it would have been during the time of the first judge Othniel. Judges 3 mentions Cushan-Rishathaim king of Aram Naharaim. Aram-Naharaim is commonly identified with Nahrima mentioned in three tablets of the Amarna Letters. It is a geographical description of the kingdom of Mitanni – which is part of modern day Northern Syria, Northern Iraq, and Eastern Turkey. Mitanni existed from approximately 1500-1300 BC. It became a regional power after the Hittite destruction of Amorite Babylon created a power vacuum in Mesopotamia, and it existed until it was annexed into the Assyrian Empire.

There is another issue with the theory that Ramesses II was the pharaoh of the Exodus, and it is due to events related to the collapse of the Bronze Age. There were significant shifts in power between circa 1200 and 1150 BC. Numerous nations or peoples were partially or destroyed, including: Hittites, Mycenaean Greeks, Troy, Canaanites, Amorites, Egyptians, and Babylon. This power vacuum allowed the Hebrews (who were already in Western Asia) and other populations to develop into organized nations.

Medinet Habu, the mortuary temple of Ramesses III, is a New Kingdom structure in Egypt. The temple is known as the source of inscribed reliefs depicting the advent and defeat of the Sea Peoples during the reign of Ramesses III. He was the second Pharaoh of the Twentieth Dynasty and is considered to be the last New Kingdom ruler to wield any substantial authority over Egypt. The Sea Peoples are thought to be a seafaring confederation of groups known to have attacked Anatolia [Turkey], Syria, Canaan, Cyprus, and Egypt prior to the Late Bronze Age collapse. The various Sea Peoples have been proposed to have originated from either Western Turkey or Southern Europe and attacked Egypt from the time of Ramesses II to the time of Ramesses III. The Second Pylon at Medinet Habu documented these Sea Peoples in Year 8 of Ramesses III.

Trevor Bryce, a Hittitologist, stated "It should be stressed that the invasions were not merely military operations, but involved the movements of large populations, by land and sea, seeking new lands to settle." Judges 4 references 900 chariots of iron – not bronze. This massive number of iron chariots suggests political instability and large military action that occurred early in the Iron Age. The period described here would be between ~1250-1150 BC. It corresponds well to Ehud and Deborah as judges of Israel in the land of Canaan, and the Ramesses Dynasty (19th & 20th) in Egypt.

King Solomon Started to Build the Temple:

King Solomon was an immensely powerful, wealthy, and influential figure. Shortly after his death, the land of Israel was split into the Northern Kingdom (Israel) and Southern Kingdom (Judah). Because of his stature, it is possible to find records from other nations. King Solomon's chronology can be checked against Babylonian and Assyrian records. This has allowed archaeologists to date some kings in a modern framework. According to the most widely used chronology, the death of Solomon would have occurred in the spring of 931 BC. According to 1 Kings 6, the temple construction started in his fourth year as king. According to 1 Kings 11, he reigned for 40 years. Based on this, Solomon would have started his reign circa 970 BC and the temple would have been started in May (Ziv / Iyar) 966 BC (which is a year of Jubilee). Based on 1 Kings 6, the Exodus would have been 480 years prior, which would date it to 1446 BC. The Passover associated with the Exodus occurred on Nisan 14 (~April 22), 1446 BC. This would date the fall of Jericho 40 years later in 1406 BC (which is also a year of Jubilee).

Exodus and the Collapse of the Middle Kingdom:

Merneferre Ay was the longest reigning Egyptian pharaoh of the Thirteenth Dynasty. He ruled a fragmented Egypt for over 23 years. Merneferre Ay is the last pharaoh of the Thirteenth Dynasty to be verified outside Upper Egypt. Despite his long reign, the number of artifacts attributable to him is comparatively small. This may point to problems in Egypt at the time. By the end of his reign, the Egyptian state seemed to have completely collapsed. Shortly after his death, the Hyksos of Western Asia moved into and gained control of Egypt. Their base of operations was a city called Avaris (This is discussed in more detail later in this chapter). For this and other reasons, some scholars consider Merneferre Ay to be the last pharaoh of the Middle Kingdom of Egypt.

According to the Book of Exodus, Egypt was exposed to numerous plagues, starvation, loss of numerous slaves, and even the loss of the pharaoh. Merneferre Ay is probably not the pharaoh that died in the Red Sea chasing the Israelites. However, he would be a guide post to that specific pharaoh. The rulers right after him only served as pharaoh for a few years. He may have been the pharaoh of Exodus 1 and 2 that killed the young male children of Israel, and whose daughter raised Moses. Moses in Hebrew means "drawn out of water". Moses in Egypt means "son of", such as Dedumose, Ahmose, and Thutmose.

The crossing of the Jordan River and the Battle of Jericho occurred in the spring of 1406 BC. Israel wandered the desert for 40 years (Numbers 32:10-13), which places the first Passover (Exodus 11-12) in 1446 BC. According to Exodus 7:7, Moses was 80 years old at the onset of the ten plagues. This would place his birth around 1526 BC.

Joseph and Pharaoh Amenemhat III

Amenemhat III was a pharaoh of the Twelfth Dynasty in the Middle Kingdom of Egypt. His reign is regarded as the golden age of the Middle Kingdom. Around Year 15 of his reign, he built a pyramid at

Hawara, near the entrance of the Fayum oasis. This is where he was eventually buried, indicating its importance. There is very little evidence for military expeditions during his reign, unlike his father (Senusret III). There is only one record for a small mission in Year 9. The evidence for that was found in a rock inscription near the fortress of Kumma. The text reports that a military mission went North with a small troop and that nobody died when going back South. Many expeditions to mining areas are recorded. Sometime during his long rule, Amenemhat III connected the Fayum Depression to the Nile River. The region had been a swamp previously. A 16 kilometers long canal was dug. It is known as Mer-Wer (the Great Canal) or Bahr Yussef (Joseph's Waterway). The area became a breadbasket for the country and continued to be used until 230 BC when the Lahun branch of the Nile River silted up. The chief crops were cereals, cotton, figs, grapes, olives, and sheep.

This canal was meant to serve three purposes: control the flooding of the Nile River, regulate the water level of the Nile River during dry seasons, and serve the surrounding area with irrigation. This region has the earliest evidence for farming in Egypt, and was a center of royal pyramid and tomb building in the Twelfth Dynasty of the Middle Kingdom, and again during the rule of the Ptolemaic Dynasty between the 4th and 2nd Centuries BC.

Amenemhat III is the most likely candidate for being the pharaoh that Joseph served under. Referring to Genesis 47, Joseph ensured that Egypt had plenty of stored grains prior to the famine. As part of this process, the leaders of Egypt would have developed ways to increase crop yields and improve warehouse storage. Bahr Yussef may bear the name of its architect - Joseph. When the famine hit, the Pharaoh was the only entity with large stores of food. It is conceivable that out of desperation, people would have sold everything they had, including themselves, just to ensure survival. Because of this, there would have been a significant shift in wealth from local power centers to a centralized government. This could explain why Amenemhat III became extremely wealthy and powerful. If Joseph was the Vizier of Egypt, he might have encouraged exploration, mining, and infrastructure development. He might have discouraged military expeditions for philosophical and religious reasons. This is consistent with the reign of Amenemhat III.

Also, Potiphar of the Bible may be Ptahwer of Egyptian history. Potiphar, as described in Genesis 37:36 and Genesis 39:1 is an officer of Pharaoh and captain of the guard. He is the one who purchased Joseph as a slave from the Midianites. In the Ancient Records of Egypt written by James Henry Breasted, Ptahwer is described as a master of the double cabinet, chief of the treasury under Amenemhat III, and born of Yata. The evidence provided in this section indicates that Amenemhat III is a strong candidate for being Joseph's pharaoh.

Joseph

Joseph has already been linked to the reign of Pharaoh Amenemhat III and the 12th Dynasty of Egypt. Most agree that Amenemhat III reigned during the 1800s BC. Many place his reign at 1860-1814 BC. We agree that Amenemhat III reigned in the 1800s BC, but not necessarily those exact years.

At an archaeological site known as Tell el-Dab'a, extensive excavations have been carried out, starting with Swiss archaeologist

Édouard Naville in 1885. Manfred Bietak of the Austrian Archaeological Institute of Cairo has been working the site since 1966. It contains residences, tombs, and temples that combine Egyptian and Canaanite architectural styles. The society of Tell el-Dab'a interacted with people from other regions. Although the site has been damaged by the environment, continual rebuilding, and agriculture, archaeologists have shown that this city was occupied by a wealthy society. Approximately 500 pieces of pottery from Cypress containing oil and perfume have been discovered. The most noteworthy temple is Temple I. It is in the Egyptian style and contains three sanctuaries. The altar in its courtyard has evidence that sacrifices may have been made. The outside walls were made of whitewashed mud-brick. Traces of blue paint have been found on the walls.

About 1 km (½ mile) northeast of Tell el-Dab'a is a small village called Ezbet Rushdi. It is a 12th Dynasty site that was partly excavated by Shehata Adam from 1951 to 1954. The Austrian Archaeological Institute re-excavated the site in 1996. It was discovered that, prior to the construction of the temple, there was already an early 12th dynasty settlement there. After looking at the floor plans and layout of the Ezbet Rushdi temple, it looks similar, although not the same, as the floor plans and layout for King Solomon's temple.

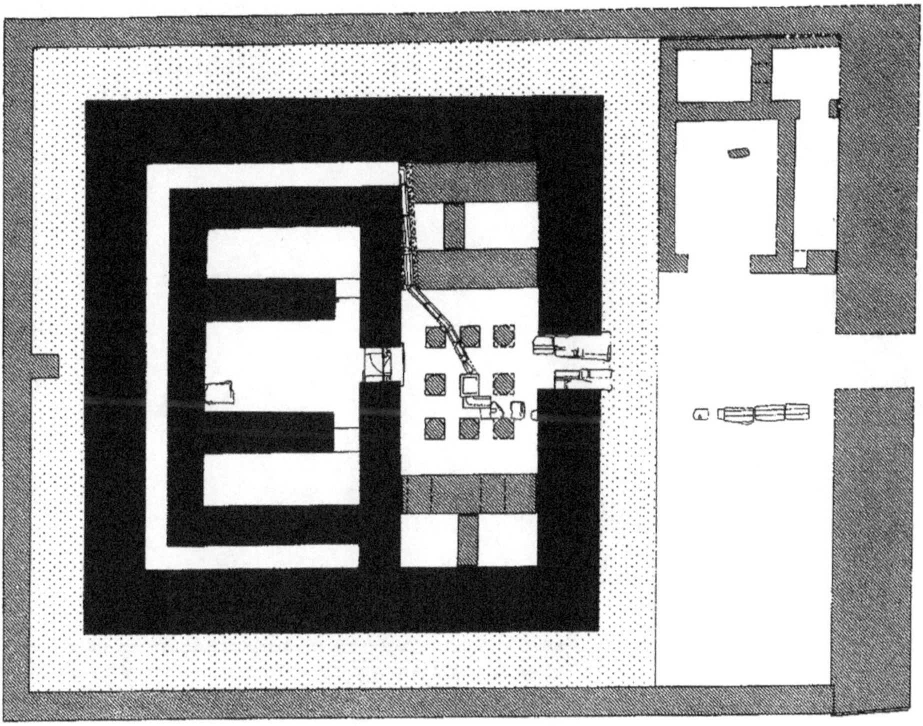

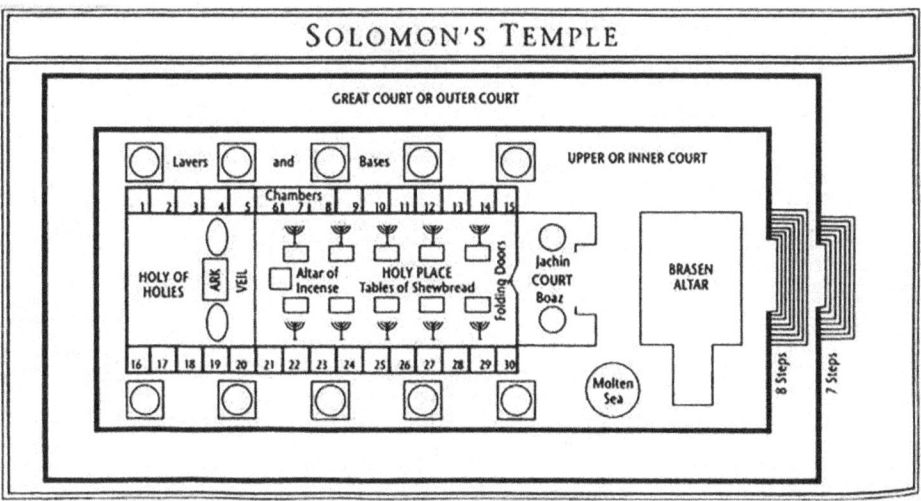

Ezbet Rushdi Temple

King Solomon's Temple

Compare these floor plans to those of Deir el-Bahari, which is the mortuary temple complex started by Nebhepetre Mentuhotep II. He is the 4th Pharaoh of the 11th Dynasty and considered the 1st Pharaoh of the Middle Kingdom. He reigned for 51 years.

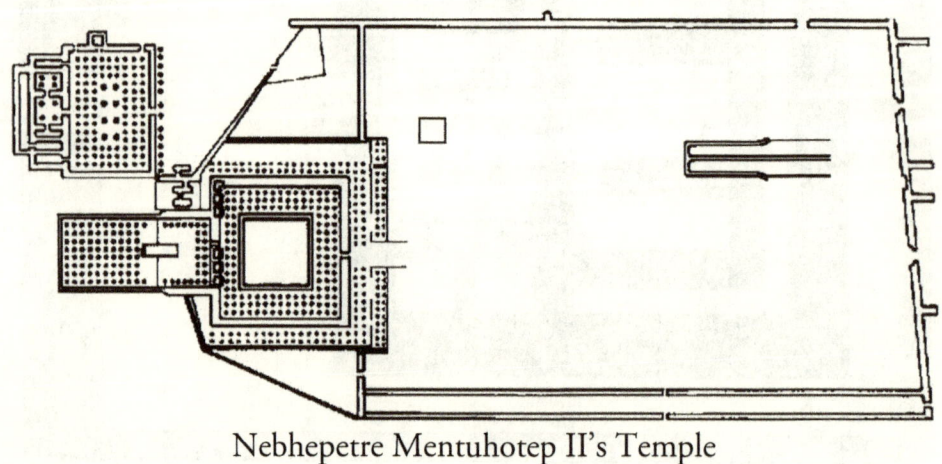

Nebhepetre Mentuhotep II's Temple

The design of the temple of Deir el-Bahari (11th Dynasty) is significantly different to that of Ezbet Rushdi (12th Dynasty). There could be numerous reasons for this, but when you compare Ezbet Rushdi to King Solomon's Temple, many similarities are observed. One of the more significant similarities is that in both Ezbet Rushdi and Solomon's Temple the inner chamber is pushed into the back of the space, whereas the inner chamber of Deir el-Bahari is in the center of the space.

Furthermore, the Tell el-Dab'a / Ezbet Rushdi complex has evidence for Asiatics in the 12th and 13th Dynasties, which is the general period when Jacob entered Egypt and the Israelites left Egypt. There was a socio-economic and cultural mix with evidence of both farming and regional trade. There were numerous enclosures that probably kept animals. Also, there are examples of Minoan artwork – who were based in Crete – which is about 650 km or 400 miles from the port city of Alexandria by boat. In one section of the settlement, the number 12 was a common attribute of the artifacts found. There was a building with 12 columns for support. In one specific area, there were 12 graves. One grave belonged to a man of some importance. It was pyramid shaped. Inside was a statue of a person with reddish hair, yellowish skin, and a multicolored robe. According to Egyptologist David Rohl, this encampment is unique in the world. There is nothing like it past or present. The complex correlates well to a Hebrew settlement (Goshen) during the 12th Dynasty that was quickly abandoned and replaced by the Hyksos capital city of Avaris in the 13th Dynasty.

It is not hard to imagine a scenario right out of Genesis and Exodus in the Bible. Jacob entered Egypt during the 12th Dynasty. They designed and built an entire community, including a temple and housing, in relative peace. When they left during the Exodus, the Hyksos took advantage of both the existing empty buildings and relative isolation. All this occurred primarily during the 12th and 13th Dynasties of the Middle Kingdom of Egypt (~1900-1400 BC).

Abraham and the 3rd Dynasty of Ur

According to Genesis 11-12, Abraham was born of Terah in Ur of the Chaldeans – which was an ancient city close to the northwest end of the Persian Gulf. He is related to Noah and Adam through Shem – making him a Shemite (aka Semitic). He lived in Canaan, Haran, and Egypt. He left Canaan for Egypt due to a severe famine.

The cities of Sodom and Gomorrah were destroyed by fire and brimstone while he was alive. He was involved in a war in the days of King Amraphel of Shinar, King Arioch of Ellasar, King Chedorlaomer of Elam, King Tidal of Goyim, King Bera of Sodom, King Birsha of Gomorrah, King Shinab of Admah, King Shemeber of Zeboiim, and King of Bela / Zoar in the Valley of Siddim (Dead Sea).

Ur of the Chaldeans was a Sumerian city located on the northwest side of the Persian Gulf close to modern day Nasiriyah, Iraq. The area between the Tigris and Euphrates Rivers is often called Mesopotamia. It has been inhabited for thousands of years and has a very rich history. Although we can reach back even further, let's start with Sargon of Akkad. He was the founder and first ruler of the Semitic speaking Akkadian Empire, which is one of the earliest known empires to exist. Akkad is referenced as Accad in Genesis 10:10. His family reigned for five generations until Shar-Kali-Sharri's death.

Succeeding his father Naram-Sin to the throne, Shar-Kali-Sharri ruled during an age of increasing troubles. The raids of the Gutian peoples from the Zagros mountains (between modern day Iraq and Iran) that began in his father's reign were becoming more and more frequent. He was faced with a number of rebellions from vassal kings against the high taxes they were forced to pay to fund the defense against the Gutian threat. Sumer (Shinar in the Bible) also suffered from a terrible drought around the same time, leading to the complete abandonment of some cities. After Shar-Kali-Sharri's death, Sumer fell into anarchy.

The Gutians practiced hit-and-run tactics. They would be long gone by the time regular troops could arrive to deal with the situation. Their raids crippled the economies of Sumer and Akkad. Travel became unsafe, as did work in the fields. The Sumerian King List (an ancient stone tablet) indicates that king Ur-Utu of Uruk (Erech in the Bible – Genesis 10:10) was defeated by the Guti. They also defeated the Akkadian army, took Akkad, and destroyed it. Akkad was so thoroughly destroyed that its site is still unknown to this day. The Guti proved to be poor rulers. They could not keep up with demands. The short-lived Gutian power crumbled and a short "dark age" swept over Mesopotamia.

The 3rd Dynasty of Ur was established when the Gutian regime fell apart. It lasted until the Elamite invasion. The Elamites were from the eastern side of the Persian Gulf. The region is now part of Iran. Sumer during this time had a cultural explosion. Archaeologists have found numerous artifacts related to law, art, culture, math, and religion. The Elamites, allied with the people of Susa and led by king Kindattu, the sixth king of Simashki, conquered Ur and captured King Ibbi-Sin, thus ending the 3rd Dynasty of Ur. However, by the time the Elamites took over, the Sumerian population had dropped by 93%. This is when the Sumerian language died out.

This time of the Akkadians, Sumerians, Gutians, and Elamites provides the backdrop for the life of Abraham. King Tidal, according to Genesis 14:1, ruled Goyim. Goyim / Goiim is the literal term used in the Masoretic text. It has been translated as people or nations, but it may be a literal term referencing the Gutian nation. It is quite possible that Goyim was a city controlled by the Gutians. No conclusive evidence has yet been found that describes the people and events of Genesis 14. However, the political and military climate described in Genesis 14 is consistent with the 3rd Dynasty of Ur.

There is another major event described during the life of Abraham. Genesis 19 tells of the destruction of Sodom and Gomorrah by fire and brimstone from the sky. Sodom, Gomorrah, Admah, Zeboiim, and Bela / Zoar were city-states in the region of the Dead Sea (Valley of Siddim in the Bible). All but one of these cities were destroyed by brimstone - Bela / Zoar. Chronologically, the destruction of these cities described in Genesis 19 took place after the war described in Genesis 14. According to Genesis 19, Lot was in Zoar, which is the most southern of the five cities. The Bible states Zoar was spared, and historical evidence substantiates this. Zoar, later called Bela, did survive the hail of fire and brimstone.

There is a theory with quite a bit of evidence that states that these cities were destroyed by a comet. If you have ever seen pictures of the 1908 Tunguska event in Siberia with a large crater and numerous flattened trees, you see firsthand the power of a comet. Celestial objects, such as comets, that hit the ground are called meteorites. Meteorites leave certain evidence behind, including shocked glass and higher concentrations of sulfur, iridium, and nickel. Shocked glass occurs through exposure of rocks to the heat and pressure of a meteorite impact. This heat and pressure changes the surrounding rocks and minerals so much that they look somewhat like a fractured window. Comets, asteroids, and meteors have much higher concentrations of trace elements, such as sulfur, iridium, and nickel, as compared to rocks found on Earth. We do see all of these features near the Dead Sea. Meteorite impacts could have also been a reason for the severe famine that coincides with the 3rd Dynasty of Ur.

Abraham and Joseph

A lot happened during and between the times of Abraham and Joseph. They are more than just names in a book. They led full and interesting lives. We have already constructed a timeline between Moses and Jesus. This section has been added to provide further patterns, context, and texture to their lives. The first thing is to develop a relative time sequence between Abraham and Joseph. The Bible is very specific in these details.

Genesis 12:4 - Abraham 75 years old when promised a child.
Genesis 21:5 - Abraham 100 years old when Isaac was born.
Genesis 25:7 - Abraham 175 years old when he died.
Genesis 25:26 - Isaac 60 years old when Jacob was born.
Genesis 26:34, Genesis 29:20,30, Genesis 31:41 - Jacob was 91 when Joseph was born.
Genesis 41:46 - Joseph was 30 years old when he rose to power.
Genesis 47:9,28 - Jacob was 130 at start of pilgrimage. Lived 147 years.
Genesis 50:22 - Joseph 110 years old when he died.

The only number listed above that is based on calculations rather than direct statement in the Bible is the age of Jacob when Joseph was born. This is based on several calculations, including the age in which Esau was married and the 14 years Jacob worked for his wives. Numerous Biblical scholars agree with this length of time as being 91 years. So, the time between the birth of Abraham and the beginning of Jacob's pilgrimage was 290 years (100+60+130), and the time between Abraham's Covenant with God and Joseph's rise to power was 206 years (25+60+91+30).

Abraham

Abraham is significantly older than Joseph. The question is by how much. According to Genesis 11-25, Abraham was born in Ur of the Chaldeans. As mentioned earlier, the Sargonic Dynasty of the Akkadian Empire predates Abraham and the 3rd Dynasty of Ur. Sargon began his reign ~2340 BC. His family reigned for five generations until Shar-Kali-Sharri's death ~2193 BC. Sumer suffered from a terrible drought that started ~2200 BC. The Sumerian King List indicates that king Ur-Utu of Uruk was defeated by the Guti ~2150 BC. They defeated the Akkadian army, took Akkad, and destroyed it ~2115 BC. The 3rd Dynasty of Ur was established ~2112 BC. It lasted until the Elamite invasion ~2004 BC. It was at this time that the Sumerian language died out.

This time of the Akkadians, Sumerians, Gutians, and Elamites provides the backdrop for the life of Abraham. The political and military climate described in Genesis 14 is consistent with a date ~2100 BC during the 3rd Dynasty of Ur.

Genesis 19 describes the destruction of Sodom and Gomorrah by fire and brimstone from the sky. Sodom, Gomorrah, Admah, Zeboiim, and Bela / Zoar were city-states in the region of the Dead Sea. All but one of these cities were destroyed by brimstone - Bela / Zoar. There is evidence that these cities were destroyed by a comet or meteorites. Every 2500 years or so the Earth passes through a part of space that is more densely packed with comets and other fragments. Some of these fragments have been meteors and meteorites. They are part of the Taurid meteor showers. Meteorites leave certain evidence behind, including shocked glass and higher concentrations of sulfur, iridium, and nickel. In fact we do see all of these features near the Dead Sea. This meteorite impact is dated to ~2000 BC.

There is evidence of several other meteorite impacts around the world around this time. The Kaali crater is a complex of 9 impact craters near the village of Kaali in Estonia. Its true date of impact is unknown, but some have dated it to around 2000 BC. Campo del Cielo refers to a group of iron meteorites found near Buenos Aires, Argentina. Their impact is dated ~2000-3000 BC. The Henbury meteorites formed a large group of impact craters in northern Australia. Their impact is dated ~2000-2400 BC. All this points to significant meteorite activity between ~2200 and 2000 BC. There are two major Taurid meteorite impact time periods: 2200-2000 BC and 400-600 AD. The earlier one dates to severe famine in the Middle East and the end of the Sumerian civilization. The second corresponds to the end of the Roman Empire and the beginning of the Dark Ages. History has shown that these are not minor events. So a comet impact somewhere between 2200 BC and 2000 BC that affected the people near the Dead Sea and caused severe widespread famine is quite plausible.

Based on evidence, the best period for Joseph is 1900-1800 BC. The best period for Abraham is 2150-2000 BC. So what does the Bible say on this matter? We have already placed the Exodus in 1446 BC. It was 290 years between the birth of Abraham and the time Jacob entered Egypt when he was 130 years old. According to Exodus 12:40, they were in Egypt for 430 years. Based on this information, we know the year in which certain events occurred:

Exodus: 1446 BC
Moses Birth: 1526 BC

Joseph Death: 1805 BC
Jacob Entered Egypt: 1876 BC
Joseph in Power: 1885 BC
Joseph Birth: 1915 BC
Jacob Birth: 2006 BC
Sodom and Gomorrah Destroyed: ~2067 BC
Genesis 14 War: 2080 BC +/- 10 years
Abraham Covenant: 2091 BC
Abraham Birth: 2166 BC

These dates line up with archaeological evidence. Joseph was in power during the 12th Dynasty in Egypt, and Abraham lived during the 3rd Dynasty of Ur in Mesopotamia.

Nimrod, Enmerkar, and the Tower of Babel (Genesis 10-11)

Egyptian archaeologist David Rohl suggests that Nimrod of the Tower of Babel is Enmerkar. Enmerkar's father was founder of the 1st Dynasty of Uruk, which replaced the 1st Dynasty of Kish. Enmerkar is credited with the invention of writing and building Eridu (oldest known city). -kar in Enmerkar means hunter. Eridu is considered the oldest city in the world and is located is southern Iraq. Dhi Qar Governorate (southern Iraq) was the heartland of the ancient civilization of Sumer, and includes the ruins of Ur, Eridu, Lagash, Larsa, Girsu, Umma, and Bad-tibira. According to the Sumerian King List, Eridu is called the city of the first kings. The Sumerian King List mentions a Great Flood. There is a growing number of scholars who state that there is significant evidence that Eridu is the remnants of the Tower of Babel.

Nimrod was king of Shinar (Sumer), the son of Cush, and great-grandson of Noah. He was a mighty hunter and a prolific builder of cities. Enmerkar may be Nimrod, and Eridu may be remnants of the Tower of Babel.

In the Beginning (Genesis 1-11)

One of the most significant apparent conflicts between Christianity and science is related to the age of the Earth and the Universe. The Bible says that creation occurred in six days. Science says the universe is approximately 15 billion years old and the Earth is approximately 4.5 billion years old. Is it possible to reconcile these differences? The short answer is yes – sort of.

Science has not quite caught up to the Bible yet, but it is getting much closer. What? You did hear that correctly. Science is in the process of proving the Bible correct. It just hasn't realized it yet. Currently, to understand the underlying mechanics of how the universe was made from a scientific perspective requires a deep understanding of physics and mathematics. It is possible to explain some of these concepts and ideas in a way that a non-scientist could relate to.

The first critical perspective is that both the Bible and science agree that time had a beginning. Where they differ at this point is how. The Bible states that God created time. Many scientists, faced with the idea that time and the entire universe were created out of nothing by a designer, are trying to find ways around this.

Science is not at fault here. Pure science is an objective approach to collecting facts and trying to explain them. Sometimes scientists get it right, and sometimes they don't. However, as we collect more facts, we get a clearer picture of what is going on. Science does have its limits though. Because it is an objective approach, meaning that it is based on what we can observe, it cannot even begin to explain the existence of something outside the universe. Science is limited to what it can observe and measure. It answers questions that begin with "What" and "How." It cannot explain motive or intent. It cannot explain "Why."

The real issue is the people behind the science. We are all broken and separated from God. Some of us look to God for answers. Others look to themselves and other broken people for answers. Science is not about creating something complicated. It is the reverse of that. If we have learned anything, pure science simplifies. It explains with clarity, especially in the world of math and physics. As we explained earlier in this chapter, when people thought that the Earth was at the center of the universe, scientists were forced to generate complicated answers to explain our observations. However, when some scientists properly explained that the Earth and other planets moved around the Sun, and that the Sun was part of a larger galaxy, the models and mathematics to explain our observations became much simpler and less complicated. Similarly, the models and mathematics that properly explain the beginning of both time and our universe should be simple.

The second critical perspective is that time is not constant. You may have heard the story which tries to explain Einstein's theory of relativity. Twins are born on Earth. One of them remains on Earth while another travels to a nearby star and back to Earth at nearly the speed of light. For the one who was traveling, approximately ten years had passed. When the traveler returned to Earth, his twin has long since died and he meets his great grandchildren. The rate of time changes depending on how fast you are moving.

The third critical perspective is that God is independent of space and time. From His perspective, the beginning of time, the end of time, the Milky Way Galaxy, and the Tadpole Galaxy are all within His reach simultaneously. God's concept of time and space are very different from our own. According to Genesis, man was not created until the 6th day. Who's sixth day is Genesis referring to? The only obvious answer is God. He was there at the beginning. Genesis 1:1 says, "In the beginning God created..." John 1:1 says, "In the beginning was the Word, and the Word was with God, and the Word was God." Jesus was present at the beginning of all things. So, going back to our original question. How do we reconcile the age of the universe between science and the Bible? The answer is that they are looking at time from different perspectives. God and Man experience time differently. Realign those perspectives and the apparent conflicts evaporate.

Science studies the present to understand the past. History uses the past to understand the present. Science is limited to our experiences and does not have all the answers. It assumes that rates and processes in the present are similar to those in the past. This assumption is incorrect. Historical evidence reveals the accuracy of the Bible. Time and processes during Creation, the Fall of Adam and Eve, and the Great Flood were vastly different than they are today. To understand this time period from a scientific point of view, we have to change our perspectives and our perceptions.

Conclusion

Based on the discussion above, there are some events we can date with good reliability. Abraham was born in 2166 BC. The Battle of Jericho occurred on Nisan 28 or about May 14, 1406 BC. The First Temple was started in May 966 BC. King Solomon died in 931 BC. Jesus was most likely born on Tishri 1 or about September 29, 2 BC and died on Nisan 14 or about April 14, 32 AD. We can link Abraham to the 3rd Dynasty of Ur, Joseph to the 12th Dynasty of Egypt, Moses to end of the 13th Dynasty of Egypt, and some of the judges of Israel with some 19th and 20th Dynasty pharaohs in Egypt. We can connect some leaders of Israel and Judah with some leaders of Assyria and Babylon.

These are pylons that place other historical events within the Bible in chronological and historical context. We have provided a good narrative supported by strong evidence. The final answer as to whether the Bible contains accurate descriptions of past people and events, however, lies in your hands. It is up to you to decide if the Bible is historically accurate or if it is just a collection of moral stories. We want to encourage you to research these things on your own. We want to challenge you to seek facts and truth. We are confident that in the end, the Word of God will reveal itself as accurate and consistent.

Chapter 6

Trials and Tribulations

*"We are always on the anvil;
by trials God is shaping us for higher things."*
- Henry Ward Beecher

Thus far we have been developing stepping stones designed to better understand the promises within God's Word. Chapters 2 and 3 demonstrate that every detail within the Holy Bible has a purpose. Every word and every number describe the many promises that God has made to us. Chapter 4 reveals God's mission and purpose through the establishment and observation of seven feasts. God established these feasts through Moses to show His direct involvement in fulfilling His promises, and four of them have already been fulfilled. Chapter 5 demonstrates that the Bible is both scientifically and historically accurate. The Bible is not a collection of moral stories and parables used to guide and mold our lives. The Bible is a supernatural message system of truth that is inspired by He who created the heavens, the Earth, and you. Its detailed accuracy, list of already fulfilled promises, authenticity, and authority give us hope and reason to believe that every promise held within will be fulfilled. Matthew 5:18 states, "For verily I say unto you, 'Till heaven and earth pass, one jot or one tittle shall in no wise pass from the law, till all be fulfilled' [KJV]."

It is one thing to understand God's promises. It is another to accept them and rely upon them. Trials and tribulations, as seen throughout the Bible, are not there to tear us away from and blame God. It is the exact opposite. They are designed to draw us closer to God.

The account of the sacrifice of Isaac by Abraham in Genesis 22 is a dramatic record of an unprecedented commandment by God for a human sacrifice. This is without parallel in that no one else had ever been commanded to do it. This also has to be put into context with Genesis 17:2,19 which state, "I will make My covenant between Me and you, and will multiply you exceedingly... Sarah your wife shall bear you a son indeed; and you shall call his name Isaac: and I will establish My covenant with him for an everlasting covenant, and with his seed after him [KJV]."

God was not tempting Abraham to do wrong. God was not instituting or condoning child sacrifice. The purpose was for Abraham to demonstrate that he trusted God completely and without hesitation. Abraham had faith that God would fulfill His promise to build a great nation through Isaac. In this passage, that faith was being tested. Something to point out here is that Isaac's faith was being tested as well. He was not a young boy during this incident. According to Genesis 22:5-7, Isaac was clearly able to communicate and have some understanding of the situation. He was capable of carrying a load of wood up to the top of Mount Moriah. If he was able to do this, he would have been old enough and strong enough to fight back... but he didn't. This was not only a demonstration of faith by Abraham, it was also a demonstration of faith by Isaac.

At the end of the day, both Abraham and Isaac passed the test. They showed resolute faith in God's promises. Would you be able to do something like this? Would you be willing to give up the one thing that means the most to you because God commanded you to? Faith is truly believing that God does not lie and that He will fulfill His promises in His time. God is not asking us to do something He cannot do Himself. He already knows and owns everything. This is about not just knowing that you are promised something. It is about the willingness to give it to God and let Him do the heavy lifting for you. James 1:12 states, "Blessed is the man who remains steadfast under trial, for when he has stood the test he will receive the crown of life, which God has promised to those who love him [ESV]."

As stated earlier in Chapter 2, Hebrew has four levels in which it communicates: literal, implied meaning, moral meaning, and hidden meanings. The literal aspect of this passage is that Abraham followed God's command. The implied meaning is that we are to have faith in God's promises. The moral meaning is that God does not lie, and we are to follow Him. We are to have faith that God will fulfill all His promises in His time. There is a hidden meaning. Genesis 22 makes a couple of interesting statements. First, verse 2 states that the event occurs in the land of Moriah. Second, verse 12 states "...you have not withheld your son, your only son from Me." Isaac was not Abraham's only son, and he was not even the first born. Remember that he has an older half-brother named Ishmael. When you run this in parallel with John 3:16, you see a much clearer picture that was only revealed after the crucifixion of Jesus Christ about two thousand years later. This is symbolic of God the Father freely offering His only Son Jesus Christ as a full and complete sacrifice for our sins. Also, Mount Moriah is a location of importance. Many things have occurred on the exact same spot. Abraham almost sacrificed Isaac (Genesis 22:2), King David built an altar to the Lord (2 Samuel 24:25), King Solomon constructed a temple to God (2 Chronicles 3:1), Nehemiah rebuilt the temple (Ezra 5:8), Jesus cleared the money changers out of the temple that King Herod rebuilt (John 2:19-20), Islamic temple Dome of the Rock was constructed in the late 7th Century AD, and another temple will be built in the future (Daniel 9:27).

Ten Plagues of Egypt

There are two periods of trials and tribulations in the Bible we would like to discuss in more detail: plagues of Egypt (Exodus) and seal-trumpet-bowl judgments (Revelation). Where the Gospels (Matthew, Mark, Luke, John) describe the first coming of Jesus Christ as the perfect sacrificial lamb, Revelation describes His second coming as warrior leader establishing His kingdom on Earth. Both are foreshadowed in the Book of Exodus written by Moses over 1400 years before Jesus Christ was even born. As described and explained throughout this book, the Bible uses history as prophecy of future events.

To truly understand the Passover as described in Exodus is to understand God's master plan. 2 Thessalonians 2:7-8 tells us that it is the Holy Spirit who restrains Satan's power on Earth. Only once the Holy Spirit, and with Him the Church, is removed will God finally deal with Satan and his followers. "For the mystery of iniquity does already work: only he who now lets will let, until he be taken out of the way. And then shall that Wicked be revealed, whom the Lord shall consume with the spirit of His mouth, and shall destroy with the brightness of His coming [KJV]."

This removal and protection of the Church before the times of tribulation is echoed several times throughout the Bible, such as in

Genesis 7 when Noah and his family were sealed in the Ark prior to the flood. There is also a second thread throughout the Bible, and that is related to the protection of the nation of Israel during the tribulation. Revelation 7:3-4 describes how the nation of Israel will be protected from the tribulations to come. "Hurt not the earth, neither the sea, nor the trees, till we have sealed the servants of our God in their foreheads. And I heard the number of them which were sealed: and there were sealed a hundred and forty and four thousand of all the tribes of the children of Israel [KJV]." This is foreshadowed in Numbers 14 when Joshua and Caleb were protected from God's judgment and allowed to enter Canaan. Also, in Joshua 6, Rahab and her family were protected from the complete destruction of Jericho. So, the protection of the Church is the fulfillment of the promises Jesus made to those who followed Him, and the protection of the Israelites is the fulfillment of the promises God made to Abraham and Moses.

We believe the ten plagues of Egypt in Exodus are intentional in how they parallel the seal-trumpet-bowl judgments in Revelation. The plagues occurred just before Israel's exodus from the bondage of Egypt. The judgments of Revelation will occur just before the fall of Babylon and the binding of Satan for 1000 years. The ten plagues are prototypes of the seal-trumpet-bowl judgments (just as Moses is an archetype of Jesus) and provide a framework to understand them.

Seal-Trumpet-Bowl Judgments

The Apostle John's vision given to him by God on the Isle of Patmos was written in the book of Revelation near the end of the 1st Century AD. It is a prophecy about how God judges the world, binds Satan, and reclaims the world. The seal, trumpet, and bowl judgments are part of this process.

The seal, trumpet, and bowl judgments are introduced in chapters 6, 8, and 15 of Revelation. There are three sets of seven judgments for a total of 21. Wrapped within these judgments are the meaning of the numbers 21, 77, and 777. There are several verses related to variations of the number seven:

- Genesis 4:24 - "If Cain shall be avenged sevenfold, truly Lamech seventy and sevenfold [KJV]."
- Genesis 5:31 - "All the days of Lamech were seven hundred seventy and seven years: and he died [KJV]."
- Matthew 18:21-22 - " Then came Peter to him, and said, 'Lord, how often shall my brother sin against me, and I forgive him? till seven times?' Jesus said unto him, 'I say not unto you, Until seven times: but, Until seventy times seven' [KJV]."

There are 21 judgments described in Revelation. Lamech lived for 777 years and died 7 years before the birth of his great-grandson Arphaxad. Lamech lived before the flood. Arphaxad was born after the flood. 77 generations are listed in Luke 3 for the genealogy of Jesus. Within the context provided by these and other Bible verses, 21, 77, and 777 are related to the mercy (77) and wrath (21, 777) poured out upon Man's wickedness by God.

Reading through the Book of Revelation, six seals are opened by Jesus Christ. When the seventh seal is opened, the trumpet judgments began. Similarly, when the seventh trumpet judgment begins, the seven bowl judgments begin. Babylon falls and Satan is bound after the seventh bowl judgment. Revelation 8:3 mentions a golden censer in association with the trumpet judgments. A censer is filled with incense and hot coals. In the process, an aromatic smoke is released. This is symbolic of the Holy Spirit. Revelation 16:1 states that a great voice was heard from the temple when the bowl judgments are poured upon the Earth. Revelation 15:8 states that the temple was filled with smoke from the glory of God and that no man could enter. The 7 seal judgments are associated with God the Son. The 7 trumpet judgments are associated with God the Holy Spirit, and the 7 bowl judgments are associated with God the Father. All three aspects of God are on display during these seal-trumpet-bowl judgments. How do these judgments relate to the 10 plagues of Egypt?

Water Into Blood

<u>First Plague</u>

Exodus 7:20 states, "Moses and Aaron did so, as the Lord commanded; and he lifted up the rod, and smote the waters that were in the river, in the sight of Pharaoh, and in the sight of his servants; and all the waters that were in the river were turned to blood [KJV]."

<u>Second Trumpet</u>

Revelation 8:8 states, "The second angel sounded, and as it were a great mountain burning with fire was cast into the sea: and the third part of the sea became blood [KJV]."

The first Egyptian plague is that of blood. The turning of water into blood was the first of the public miracles that Moses did in Egypt

(Exodus 7:20). Even though Jesus says in John 2:4 that His time has not yet come. We think that it is intentional and consistent that turning water into wine was the first of the public miracles that Jesus did in the world (John 2:11). The turning of water to blood started the journey in which Moses led his people out of bondage toward the promised land. The turning of water into wine symbolized the journey in which Jesus took His people out of corruption and into everlasting life in freedom and liberty with God (Romans 8:21). This concept of Jesus offering living water as an alternative to death is described in John 4:5-10, John 7:37-39, and Revelation 7:16-17. The river of blood is symbolic of death, but the water into wine is symbolic of life.

Frogs

Second Plague

Exodus 8:3 states, "The river shall bring forth frogs abundantly, which shall go up and come into your house, and into your bedchamber, and upon your bed, and into the house of your servants, and upon your people, and into your ovens, and into your kneading troughs [KJV]."

Sixth Bowl

Revelation 16:13 states, "I saw three unclean spirits like frogs come out of the mouth of the dragon, and out of the mouth of the beast, and out of the mouth of the false prophet [KJV]."

The second Egyptian plague is that of frogs. These frogs in both instances are symbolic for being unclean. In the Old Testament, the frogs came from a dead river full of blood. In the New Testament, they are literally called unclean spirits. Matthew 12:43 states, "When the unclean spirit is gone out of a man, he walks through dry places, seeking rest, and finds none [KJV]." This reference goes beyond needing a bath. It conveys a whole generation of people that displays unrepentant self-absorbed wickedness. 2 Timothy 3:1-5 describes the sins and wickedness of mankind.

"In the last days perilous times shall come. For men shall be lovers of their own selves, covetous, boasters, proud, blasphemers, disobedient to parents, unthankful, unholy, without natural affection, trucebreakers, false accusers, incontinent, fierce, despisers of those that are good, traitors, heady, highminded, lovers of pleasures more than lovers of God; having a form of godliness, but denying the power thereof: from such turn away [KJV]."

Is there any relationship between the wickedness described here and the Seal-Trumpet-Bowl Judgments described in Revelation? Just as Moses (to Egypt) and Jonah (to Nineveh) were sent to give messages of repentance, so too was Jesus sent for a similar purpose. Those who turned away from God and lived wicked lives, such as those in Egypt, Sodom, Jericho, and even Jerusalem, eventually had to face captivity or destruction. Those who listened to the Word of God and turned away from their wicked ways were protected from destruction, such as Nineveh and Christians.

The remaining Egyptian plagues: lice, flies, pestilence, boils / sores, hail, locusts, darkness, and death are the result of not turning away from sin and wickedness.

The Passover Lamb

The Passover Lamb, as described in Exodus 12, foreshadows the sacrifice Jesus made to cleanse us of our sins, as described in John 1:29. "The next day John saw Jesus coming unto him, and said, 'Behold the Lamb of God, which takes away the sin of the world [KJV].'"

In Exodus 12, the Hebrews were preparing themselves for their Exodus from Egypt and captivity. God commanded them to slaughter a year-old sheep or goat on the 14th day of the first month (Nisan). They were to place its blood on the outside doorposts of their homes.

Jesus as a sacrificial lamb was also alluded to in the narrative of Abraham and Isaac above.

As described above, Genesis 22:2 states, "Take now your son, your only son Isaac, whom you love, and get yourself into the land of Moriah; and offer him there for a burnt offering upon one of the mountains which I will tell you of [KJV]." There are a couple of important points to emphasize. First, Genesis 22:2 parallels John 3:16 in that they mention the sacrifice of an only male child as a sign of love and obedience. Second, both events occurred in the exact same location – Mt Moriah – approximately 2000 years apart. Mt Moriah is also the location of King Solomon's Temple.

The time between the lives of Abraham and King Solomon is about 1000 years. The time between King Solomon and Jesus Christ is about 1000 years. Revelation 20 states that Satan will be bound for a thousand years. These thousand year increments described are not coincidences. We have stated earlier that numbers mean something in the Bible, and this is no different. A thousand in the Bible points to achievement of completeness by God. Abraham's almost sacrifice of Isaac, Solomon's Temple, and the crucifixion of Jesus Christ are all part of demonstrating and creating the kingdom that God will build on Earth in Christ's second coming.

The Passover points to the sacrifice Jesus made to restore our ability to have a relationship with God. The Passover is also a point in history where the Hebrew survived the plagues and started their journey to the Promised Land. It took another 480 years for the temple to be built in the Promised Land. Similarly, we as followers of Christ are just at the beginning of our journey when we accept Him as our Savior. We turn away from sin, evil, selfishness, and wickedness – which all eventually lead to spiritual death (as described by the plagues). We then turn toward God. We spend the rest of our lives learning and growing. Matthew 6:33 states, " Seek ye first the kingdom of God, and His righteousness; and all these things shall be added unto you [KJV]." It is our duty and honor as Christians to follow Christ's example. It is our role to demonstrate God's transformation of us from wicked unhappy selfish unbelievers destined for death to joyous loving self-sacrificing believers destined for eternal life.

Chapter 7

Servant Leadership

*"One of the great ironies of life is this:
He or she who serves almost always
benefits more than he or she who is served."*
- Gordon B. Hinckley

Both Moses and Jesus were servant leaders. Being a servant leader is demonstrating an effective blend of servant and leader. A servant serves, a leader leads. However, it is so much more than that. A servant serves joyfully and without ceasing. 1 Corinthians 9:19-23 says this about servant-hood, "For though I be free from all men, yet have I made myself servant unto all, that I might gain the more. And unto the Jews I became as a Jew, that I might gain the Jews; to them that are under the law, as under the law, that I might gain them that are under the law; to them that are without law, as without law, that I might gain them that are without law. To the weak became I as weak, that I might gain the weak: I am made all things to all men, that I might by all means save some. And this I do for the gospel's sake, that I might be partaker thereof with you [KJV]."

It is through selfless service and authentic leadership that you gain the trust of others which can be used to accomplish great things. Servant leadership is a type of authentic leadership. Based primarily on the servant leadership of Jesus Christ and His followers, over 30% of the world's population is Christians. Also, about 100 million

Bibles are sold or given away every year worldwide. The Holy Bible is the most widely printed and distributed book in the history of the world. So why is servant leadership so effective?

Authentic Leadership

An important aspect of servant leadership is the development of trust between the leader and the person being led. To be an effective servant leader is to develop trust through service. Servant leadership is one type of authentic leadership, which also includes team leadership, coaching leadership, visionary leadership, and relationship oriented leadership. So, what is authentic leadership and what are the attributes of a servant leader that are effective in generating positive results?

Randy King and I, Michael Beaumont, have written five books together about authentic leadership:

• Left-Center-Right: What is Best for America?
• Is Anybody Listening? Real Teens - True Stories - Young People Hoping to Make a Difference
• Duplicitous: How We the People Can Reclaim America
• Leading America: The Authentic Leader's Guide to Life, Liberty & the Pursuit of Happiness
• Dream 2 Achieve: Steps for Developing Today's Youth for Tomorrow's Leadership

Randy King is a leader within America's small business and membership driven communities, and has been a senior leader with the US Chamber of Commerce and National Write Your Congressman. He has also consulted with numerous CEO's of

Fortune 500 companies, National Federation of Independent Business, and the US Green Chamber of Commerce. This section provides a brief overview of authentic leadership and how it is effective. The books listed above are available for those who want to learn more about authentic leadership.

Warren Bennis, an organizational consultant, described "Leadership as the capacity to translate vision into reality." It is about the ability to turn an abstract idea into something physical and concrete. To be a leader is to have a clear idea of what you want to accomplish and leverage your influence (not power) to achieve those desired results. To be an authentic leader is to have a clear idea of what you want to accomplish and leverage your influence generated through trust to achieve those desired results. So what is the difference between influence and power, and how is this trust generated?

You are in a crowded restaurant and you need to find the person in charge. How do you identify that person? Is it by clothing or a name tag? Is it by finding the loudest person in the room? Is it by identifying the most active person in the room? Is it by the confidence and charisma a person exudes? Have you ever noticed that sometimes an assistant manager can motivate the staff better than the executive manager? This is an example of the difference between power and influence. The executive manager has the power based upon his title and position. This authority is supported by the owners who sign the paychecks. The assistant manager has gained influence because he has taken the time to develop personal and professional relationships with the employees. This person motivates and delegates based on the trust that has been developed over time.

A book that Randy King and I wrote – Leading America – describes the 3 T's of your leadership philosophy: truth, trust, and tactics. The book states that "Truth is the FOUNDATION of your personal philosophy." This statement is not incorrect, but it does not go far enough. Truth is God's foundation that all aspects of your life are based upon. Truth is the foundation of our reality, and God is the author of truth (see Chapter 1). To be truthful is to live a life based on honesty, character, and integrity. To be truthful is to reveal God's light that resides within you.

To be dishonest is to be in dissonance or disharmony with God. When you lie, cheat, or steal, you are out of alignment with God's will and plan for your life. When you are in a state of sin, it is like running really fast on a treadmill. You work very hard, but end up where you started. When you are in alignment with God's reality and His will, life becomes easier and more fulfilled.

"Have you not known? Have you not heard, that the everlasting God, the Lord, the Creator of the ends of the earth, faints not, neither is weary? There is no searching of His understanding. He gives power to the faint; and to them that have no might he increases strength. Even the youths shall faint and be weary, and the young men shall utterly fall: but they that wait upon the Lord shall renew their strength; they shall mount up with wings as eagles; they shall run, and not be weary; and they shall walk, and not faint." Isaiah 40:28-31 [KJV]

Trust is the firm belief in the reliability, truth, ability, or strength of someone or something. Trust is built upon truth. One cannot have trust without engendering truth. It is built upon the idea that a person being entrusted will be honest and will fulfill his promises. The question to ask is did God make promises, and did He fulfill them. There are literally thousands of promises in the Bible. Many of these promises are related to the first coming of Jesus Christ. Every single one of those promises has been fulfilled. Also, all the promises have been fulfilled precisely the way they were written. Do you know of anyone else who made thousands of promises, and fulfilled every single one of them precisely when and how they were described? What are some of the promises or covenants God has made to us?

The third "T" is tactics. Tactics are strategies and techniques used to accomplish specific objectives. The Bible is very clear as to what God's purpose is and how He plans to achieve it. Man sinned in the Garden of Eden (Genesis 3). Because of this, we are all sinful and separated from God (Romans 3:23). Jesus restored us and gave us the opportunity once again to be in fellowship with God (Colossians 1:20). Jesus was very clear of His expectations of us. Matthew 16:24-25 states, "If any man will come after me, let him deny himself, and take up his cross, and follow Me. For whosoever will save his life shall lose it: and whosoever will lose his life for My sake shall find it [KJV]." His message of humble service to others is consistent throughout the Bible. Humility or humbleness is about being courteous and respectful of others. It is the opposite of aggressiveness, arrogance, and selfishness. It is about putting the needs of others before your own. Humility dissipates anger and heals wounds. It allows us to see value and worth in others beyond "what is in it for me."

The second consistent message in the Bible, which is directly related to the first, is the message of love. Love is not a noun. Love is not an emotion. Love is the actions of selfless and humble service to others. Where humility is about your state of mind, love is about what you do while you are in that state of mind. Jesus had the power to destroy entire nations. Instead, He chose to be a humble servant of others and perform selfless acts. He relinquished His power, but in the process, He gained in influence.

Psalm 78:72 states, "He fed them according to the integrity of his heart; and guided them by the skillfulness of his hands [KJV]." The true spirit of authentic leadership is the mindset that all people have enormous value. It is an attitude and approach to life that actively seeks positive change in yourself and others through acts of character, courage, consistency, and compassion.

7 Attributes of a Servant Leader

1. Cultivate a culture of trust.

Great leadership is reflected by the trust and confidence your team has in you. If they trust you, they will go above and beyond to assist you. Trust and confidence is built on honesty, transparency, clarity, consistency, humility, and authenticity. Say what you mean and mean what you say. Be steadfast and consistent in your values, words, and actions. What are your values, and what do you believe in?

"He that is faithful in that which is least is faithful also in much: and he that is unjust in the least is unjust also in much." - Luke 16:10 [KJV]

2. Engage in dialogue.

Dialogue is a conversation between two people. There are numerous examples of Jesus having conversations with people. One that comes to mind is with the Samaritan woman at the well (John 4). Jesus talked to those who were willing to listen. He did not force His ideas and beliefs on others through deceit, manipulation, or coercion. He spoke with clarity of purpose. He was confident, honest, and direct. He said what needed to be said, and His actions were consistent with His words. Are your thoughts, words, and actions consistent with each other?

"Whosoever drinks of this water shall thirst again: but whosoever drinks of the water that I shall give him shall never thirst; but the water that I shall give him shall be in him a well of water springing up into everlasting life." - John 4:13-14 [KJV]

3. Value diversity.

Diversity has several cultural meanings. The Biblical concept of diversity does not mean that everyone can define right and wrong for themselves. The law given to Moses defines right and wrong. Diversity in the context of being a follower of Christ is about the concept that you have value and can be valuable regardless of your age, gender, ethnicity, quality of health, or social status. How do you find value in others?

"Come unto me, all ye that labor and are heavy laden, and I will give you rest." - Matthew 11:28 [KJV]

4. Set and follow through on expectations.

A component of effective leadership is the ability to set expectations, ensure that all involved understand those expectations, and hold everyone – including yourself – accountable to those expectations.

With that in mind, what does it mean to be a Christian? There are many variations on this, but at its core, there is one singular truth about being a Christian. As a follower of Christ, you recognize that you are sinful and are separated from God by that sin. You understand that Christ sacrificed Himself as a sinless substitute to remove all our sins to create a bridge between God and ourselves. You also know that this is a gift of God through grace and not something that can ever be earned. What is one expectation God has of you?

"For by grace are you saved through faith; and that not of yourselves: it is the gift of God: not of works, lest any man should boast."
- Ephesians 2:8-9 [KJV]

5. Be a problem solver.

On a good day life is messy. We often must make some difficult choices and are faced with many challenges. You cannot put effective leadership in a box and forget about it. An effective leader provides opportunities for personal growth and development. An effective leader transforms your way of thinking in many aspects of your life. How one solves a problem in one situation can be applied to many others in the future. Being an effective servant leader is about providing supervised opportunities that encourage a person to learn both personal and professional skills that encourage long-term growth. Do you have someone close to you that you learn from?

"Therefore if any man be in Christ, he is a new creature: old things are passed away; behold, all things are become new." - 2 Corinthians 5:17 [KJV]

6. Develop other leaders.

When it was time for Jesus to start His ministry, the first thing He did was get baptized. The second thing He did was to be tempted in the wilderness by Satan. The third thing He did was to gather disciples who would be future leaders. He did not reveal Himself to the masses. Instead, He worked with and trained a select few who would be able to lead others the way He led them. What process did Jesus use to train His disciples?

A. Selection: He chose a few ordinary, but faithful men that were trainable. He focused His attention on a select few so that He could concentrate His efforts.

B. Association: His disciples, or leaders-in-training, were with Jesus all the time. Jesus simply asked them to "follow Him."

C. Commitment: Jesus called His disciples to turn away from their own selfish desires and to commit themselves to Him. Likewise, Jesus committed Himself fully to their training.

D. Demonstration: Jesus taught through a consistency of both words and action. He practiced what He preached. His disciples learned how to be like Christ by watching and learning.

E. Delegation: As His disciples grew in experience and understanding, He put them to work by giving them specific tasks and duties.

F. Supervision: He closely monitored His disciples and used their experiences to instruct them further.

G. Reproduction: Jesus started with the end in mind. His goal was to generate disciples who could generate other disciples.

"Go ye therefore, and teach all nations, baptizing them in the name of the Father, and of the Son, and of the Holy Ghost: teaching them to observe all things whatsoever I have commanded you: and, lo, I am with you always, even unto the end of the world" – Matthew 28:19-20 [KJV]. Are you being a true disciple of Jesus by training others to follow Him?

7. Think long-term.

God transcends time and space. All is known before it ever happens. God's purpose for creating the universe is to have a permanent relationship with you. Do you have a regular time set aside to pray to God and read His Word?

"Before I formed you in the belly I knew you; and before you came forth out of the womb I sanctified you, and I ordained you a prophet unto the nations." - Jeremiah 1:5 [KJV]

Moses as a Servant Leader

The story of Moses as a servant leader starts at the burning bush (Exodus 3). The most important aspect of this event is how Moses responded. God called to Moses, and Moses responded with "Here I am." To be a servant leader is to be a humble person of action with a specific purpose. In this case, Moses was to lead the Israelites out of the bondage of Egypt and to the Promised Land.

This was not going to be easy. Egypt had one of the mightiest military in the world at the time. Moses, however, was uniquely trained for this purpose. The first 40 years of his life was spent as a prince of Egypt. He was a member of Pharaoh's court, and as such, he would have learned Egyptian customs, policies, administration, and military practices. He would have been taught how to read and write. He would have observed the inner workings of Egyptian government and leadership.

The second 40 years of his life were spent in the land of the Midianites, which is in the general region of Saudi Arabia and Jordan. This is the same area that the Israelites moved around in after they left the land of Egypt. This means that Moses was quite familiar with that region. Even though this would have been unfamiliar territory for most of the Israelites, Moses would have known sources of water, caravan trails, tribal leaders, and much more. So what was the leadership style of Moses like?

In Exodus 2, we understand that Moses is a flawed man in that he killed an Egyptian. When a leader does something morally wrong, that action can prevent him from being an effective leader. A leader's actions must be consistent with his words. In Exodus 3, we see that God calls us to serve where we are at. It's not about being perfect or fixing ourselves first. It's about becoming a better version of ourselves by serving the needs of others. In Exodus 6, Moses was honest about his imperfections. This is not about allowing our inabilities to stop us. It is about demonstrating faith by allowing God to turn our problems into His solutions. In Exodus 15, Moses was the one who listened to the problems and the criticisms. There was no water. Moses listened to his people and turned to God for a solution. In Exodus 18, we see that Moses had a close trusted confidant in Jethro. It is important to find someone that can help keep you accountable and offer support. It is also important to be teachable. We also see in Exodus 18, that Moses acted upon Jethro's advice and developed a system to develop and empower others to support the process of governance. Moses enshrined the laws for the people of Israel to follow in the books of Leviticus and Deuteronomy.

Time, Talents, and Treasure

There is another set of 3 T's that are important for the Christian to understand, and that is the giving of our time, talents, and treasure. We are called to be good stewards. Stewardship is about supervising or managing people and resources. It has nothing to do with actual ownership. There are four elements related to the concept and action of stewardship.

Good Stewardship

A) Principle of Ownership

Psalm 24:1 states, "The earth is the Lord's, and the fullness thereof; the world, and they that dwell therein [KJV]." God owns everything. We are managers or administrators acting on His behalf. Stewardship is the commitment of one's self and possessions to God's service, recognizing that we do not have the right of control over our property or ourselves.

B) Principle of Responsibility

Genesis 2:15 states, "The Lord God took the man, and put him into the garden of Eden to dress it and to keep it [NKJV]." Owners have rights. Stewards have responsibilities. We are called as God's stewards to manage that which belongs to God. He has graciously entrusted us with the care, development, and enjoyment of everything He owns. We are to manage His holdings well and according to His desires and purposes.

C) Principle of Accountability

Like the servants in the Parable of the Talents (Matthew 25:14-30), we will be called to give an account of how we have administered everything we have been given, including our time, money, abilities, information, wisdom, relationships, and authority.

D) Principle of Reward

Colossians 3:23-24 states, "Whatsoever you do, do it heartily, as to the Lord, and not unto men; knowing that of the Lord you shall receive the reward of the inheritance: for you serve the Lord Christ [KJV]." We need to be faithful stewards of all God has given us. We are not rewarded by our works alone, but by our works through faith. James 2:17-20,24 states, "Even so faith, if it has not works, is dead, being alone. Yea, a man may say, 'You have faith, and I have works: show me your faith without your works, and I will show you my faith by my works. You believe that there is one God; you do well: the devils also believe, and tremble. But will you know, O vain man, that faith without works is dead? ...You see then how that by works a man is justified, and not by faith only [KJV]."

How to Give

A) We are expected and required to give.

Jesus said to His disciples in Matthew 6:2, "when you do charitable deeds..." Jesus does not say "if," He says "when." Charitable giving is an essential part of being Christian and being Christ-like. Jesus also says in Matthew 16:24, "If any man will come after me, let him deny himself, and take up his cross, and follow Me [KJV]."

B) We are to give for the right reasons.

Jesus warned His disciples not to give for the sake of being admired by men. Matthew 6:1 states, "Take heed that you do not your charitable deeds before men, to be seen of them: otherwise you have no reward of your Father which is in heaven [KJV]." Our motives for giving are to honor God, not to honor ourselves among men. Charitable giving is to be in line with God's will and purpose.

C) We are to give as an act of worship.

Matthew 6:21 states, "For where your treasure is, there will your heart be also [KJV]." God understands that where we spend our time and our money, our hearts will also be there. God wants us to be cheerful givers (2 Corinthians 9:6-7) so that we do not miss out on the true joy of being Christ-like. Tithing and charitable giving according to God's will and purpose align our desires with His.

D) We are to give according to our means.

The Apostle Paul states in 2 Corinthians 8:12, "For if there be first a willing mind, it is accepted according to that a man has, and not according to that he has not [KJV]." We should give in proportion to what God has given us. As we have more, we should give more. 2 Corinthians 9:6 states, "He which sows sparingly shall reap also sparingly; and he which sows bountifully shall reap also bountifully [KJV]."

E) We are to be cheerful givers.

2 Corinthians 9:7 states, "Every man according as he purposes in his heart, so let him give; not grudgingly, or of necessity: for God loves a cheerful giver [KJV]." We are to have deliberate resolve to give cheerfully. God does not need our money. He wants our hearts. Where you spend your money reveals that state of your heart. Are you there to love God and help others, or are you there to please yourself?

F) We are to give of our first fruits.

Proverbs 3:9 states, "Honor the Lord with your substance, and with the firstfruits of all your increase [KJV]." First fruit sacrifices had to do with God's expectation that His people should always set aside the first part of their crops and produce as thanksgiving for His goodness. Also, these first fruits ought to be unblemished and the best available.

What to Give

When you see a person on the side of the road asking for money, what is your first response? Is it to throw a few coins in their cup? Is it to walk past and ignore them?

How did Jesus give of Himself? The short answer is that He gave everything not expecting anything in return. His primary purpose was to die as a perfect sacrifice for our sins. This is sacrificial love. It is the willingness to share your biggest and best strengths with others.

None of us are called to give in the same ways. Those who are retired or unemployed may be called to give of our time. Those who have professional education and experience may be called to give of our talents. Those who have done financially well in life may be called to give of our treasure. Tithes and offerings are not about writing a check to a church on a regular basis and calling it a day. At their core, giving of time, talents, and treasure are about investing ourselves through service and humility into the lives of others – our neighbors.

So who are our neighbors? We are not expected to help everyone everywhere. We are expected to help those around us who can be of use to the help we can provide. If you are a singer... sing. If you are a writer... write. If you are a teacher... teach. If you are a healer... heal. Give of yourself joyfully and completely. Be the best giver that you can be. By becoming servant leaders and joyful givers, we become more like Christ, and we develop more faith, hope, and love.

Christian Connectors

Christian Connectors is a registered 501(c)3 non-profit organization based in Indiana. Its dual purpose is to provide networking opportunities for Christian business leaders & professionals, and to provide opportunities to learn how to serve others through our time, talents, and treasures. You can find more information about them at http://christianconnectors.org/.

Chapter 8

Parallels

"In contemplation and reverie, one thought introduces another perpetually; and it is by similarity, or the hooking of one upon the other, that the process of thinking is carried on."
- William Godwin

Moses is an archetype or an example of Jesus. This book connects some of the ideas in the Old Testament as seen through the life of Moses with ideas in the New Testament as seen through the life of Jesus. Whereas Moses was a man and a servant of God who led the Israelites out of bondage from Egypt, Jesus is both God and Man who allowed Himself to be crucified on the cross to pay for our sins in order to restore our relationship with God.

Feasts

We have already discussed how the 7 feasts described in Leviticus 23 represent the work of Jesus on Earth during His first and second coming. It is Moses who described the necessity to honor and celebrate these feasts. They tell a singular story. Jesus was crucified as the perfect sacrificial lamb for our sins. He was buried and was resurrected on the third day. 40 days later, he ascended into heaven. Seven weeks and one day after He was crucified, the Holy Spirit became our redeemer and companion. At the end of times, the Earth will be cleansed and God will restore His kingdom on Earth.

Parallels

On Nisan 10, a lamb without blemish shall be presented as a sacrifice (Exodus 12:3). On Nisan 10, Jesus was presented as the Messiah who was later crucified (John 12:12-13).

A lamb without blemish shall be kept until the 14th day of Nisan. The congregation of Israel shall kill it at twilight (Exodus 12:5-6). Jesus, who was perfect and sinless, was handed over by the Israelites to Roman officials to be crucified. He died on Nisan 14 or Passover (Matthew 27:1-2, 1 Peter 1:18-19).

Feast of Unleavened Bread occurred in relationship to Passover. It is the removal of yeast (symbolic for sin and decay) from the household and represents cleansing (Exodus 12:14-20). Jesus performs the breaking of bread during the Feast of Unleavened Bread. It is a new covenant related to the sanctification of us through the sacrifice of Jesus Christ (Matthew 26:26-28).

Bones of the Passover lamb were not to be broken (Exodus 12:46). The bones of Jesus were not broken while on the cross (John 19:31-33).

Moses parted the Red Sea on Nisan 17 to save the Israelites from the bondage of Egypt (Exodus 14). Jesus was resurrected on Nisan 17 to save us all from the bondage of sin (Matthew 12:40).

Redemption concerning those in bondage (Exodus 21:1-11). Redemption by Jesus concerning those in bondage to sin (Ephesians 1:3-14).

A lamb shall be offered at twilight along with a grain and drink offering (Exodus 29:41). Jesus offered bread and drink to the disciples the evening before He was to be crucified (Luke 22:14-23).

Feast of First fruits is on Nisan 17 (Leviticus 23:10-14). Resurrection of Jesus Christ occurred on Nisan 17 (Matthew 27:62-66 , 28:1-6).

History

Moses was raised as a prince in the land of Egypt. Jesus was raised as the son of a carpenter in land controlled by the Roman Empire. We developed a compelling narrative to provide historical background and context for the people and events surrounding the lives of Jesus and Moses.

<u>Parallels</u>

Moses was born while Israel was in bondage to Egypt (Exodus 1:8-11). Jesus was born while Israel was in bondage to Rome (Luke 2:1).

Pharaoh killed all the male children of Israel (Exodus 1:22). Herod killed all the male children under two years old in and around Bethlehem (Matthew 2:16).

Moses was hidden for three months in Egypt to avoid being killed (Exodus 2:2). Jesus was hidden in Egypt to avoid being killed (Matthew 2:13).

Moses was drawn out of the water (Exodus 2:10). Jesus was drawn out and baptized by water (Matthew 3:16).

Moses spent part of his life away from the spotlight in Midian (Exodus 2:15). Jesus spent part of his life away from the spotlight in Nazareth (Matthew 2:23).

Plagues

Where the Gospels (Matthew, Mark, Luke, John) describe the first coming of Jesus Christ as the perfect sacrificial lamb, Revelation describes His second coming as warrior leader establishing His kingdom on Earth. Both are foreshadowed in the Book of Exodus written by Moses. The ten plagues of Egypt in Exodus are intentional in how they parallel the seal-trumpet-bowl judgments in Revelation. The plagues occurred just before Israel's exodus from the bondage of Egypt. The judgments of Revelation will occur just before the fall of Babylon and the binding of Satan for 1000 years. The ten plagues associated with Moses are prototypes of the seal-trumpet-bowl judgments associated with the second coming of Christ.

Parallels

Moses was called to bring the Israelites out of the bondage of Egypt (Exodus 3:10). Jesus was sent to set free all people from the bondage of sin (Luke 4:18).

The Israelites were brought out of the bondage of Egypt by great judgments (Exodus 7:4). God will put an end to the bondage of sin through seven last plagues (Revelation 15:1).

Water is turned into blood by Moses (Exodus 7:17). Water is turned into wine by Jesus (John 2:9). Water is turned into blood by the second angel of the Holy Spirit (Revelation 8:8).

The river shall bring forth frogs (Exodus 8:3). Unclean spirits like frogs shall come out of the mouths of the dragon, the beast, and the false prophet (Revelation 16:13).

There is pestilence associated with the plagues (Exodus 9:3). There is pestilence associated with the judgments (Revelation 6:8).

There are sores associated with the plagues (Exodus 9:10). There are sores associated with the judgments (Revelation 16:2).

There is hail associated with the plagues (Exodus 9:23). There is hail associated with the judgments (Revelation 8:7).

There are locusts associated with the plagues (Exodus 10:4). There are locusts associated with the judgments (Revelation 9:3).

There is darkness associated with the plagues (Exodus 10:1). There is darkness associated with the judgments (Revelation 16:10).

There is death associated with the plagues (Exodus 11:5). There is death associated with the judgments (Revelation 6:8).

Leadership

Both Moses and Jesus were servant leaders. It is through selfless service and authentic leadership that you gain the trust of others which can be used to accomplish great things. The story of Moses as a servant leader starts at the burning bush. The most important aspect of this event is how Moses responded. God called to Moses, and Moses responded with "Here I am." Moses was a flawed man, but he was willing to follow God. Because of this, the Israelites were led out of the bondage of Egypt and eventually into the freedom of the Promised Land by his successor – Joshua. Based primarily on the servant leadership of Jesus Christ and His followers, over 30% of the world's population is Christians. Also, about 100 million Bibles are sold or given away every year worldwide. The Holy Bible is the most widely printed and distributed book in the history of the world.

Parallels

Moses was a shepherd (Exodus 3:1). Jesus is the good shepherd (John 10:11).

Moses enlisted and trained others to help with his mission (Exodus 18:13-24). Jesus enlisted and trained others to help with His mission (Matthew 4:18-22).

Altar of worship to be built of natural materials made by God, not of objects made by man (Exodus 20:22-26). We are to deny ourselves and our own works and follow Christ (Matthew 16:24-28).

You should be willing to help those in need (Deuteronomy 15:7-11). How you treated those with the least is how you treated Me (Matthew 25:37-40).

Other

Moses met Zipporah, a Midianite woman, at a well that became his bride (Exodus 2:15-21). Even though Moses was raised as a prince in Pharaoh's court, he was willing to help women he did not know. He defended them against other men who were giving them problems, and he watered their animals. Jesus met a Samaritan woman at a well that became part of His church – aka His bride (John 4:6-15). Even though Jesus is the Son of God, He was willing to talk to an immoral non-Jewish woman. The woman did not truly understand Jesus' purpose or meaning when He talked to her about living water. She asked for some of this living water out of faith not truly understanding exactly what she was asking. Followers of Christ are often called His bride. Both Moses and Jesus found a bride at the well.

God said to Moses that He is the God of Abraham and "I am who I am" (Exodus 3:14). God may be pointing out that He is eternal and self-existent. He may also be reminding Moses of His promises to Abraham. Jesus said to the Jews, "Before Abraham was I am" (John 8:58). Similarly, Jesus may be pointing out that He is eternal and self-existent. He may also be reminding the Jews of His promises to Abraham.

Israelites fed with manna and quail from heaven (Exodus 16). Jesus fed the multitudes with fish and bread (Matthew 14:13-21, Matthew 15:32-39). The common theme in both passages is that God provides. He understands more than we do that food, clothing, and shelter are necessities. It has also been pointed out in the Bible, such as in Matthew 6:33, that we are to rely on God and seek Him first. A similar parallel is that of Exodus 36:2-7 (Those involved in building God's house brought more than enough to build the house) and Matthew 6:25-34 (God provides what is needed). This reinforces that God has promised to provide what is needed to those who believe in Him and follow His will and purpose.

Moses struck a rock and water flowed out of it for the Israelites to drink (Exodus 17:1-7). The side of Jesus was pierced and water came out (John 19:31-37). Jesus has been called the cornerstone and the rock of our salvation. We are saved through His sacrifice and resurrection. Moses struck the rock to bring forth water which parallels the Roman soldier piercing the side of Jesus and water being released. Also, the Israelites were in a desert. There was no water. Unlike an oasis where there is much vegetation and life, there is not abundant life in the desert. By relying on God and His promise to lead them to the Promised Land, Moses demonstrated his own faith and he demonstrated God's power, love, and grace by bringing forth life sustaining water in the middle of a desert.

God gave the Ten Commandments to Moses (Exodus 20:1-17). Jesus stated the 2 commandments to the Pharisees (Matthew 22:34-40). God gave the law to Moses, and Moses wrote the laws down for the Israelites (Deuteronomy 27:1-10). The 10 Commandments, and the other laws, given to Moses clearly defined what sin is and the consequences of them. God also provided laws to provide guidance to maintain a healthy society (Exodus 21-23, Leviticus 11-15, 18). Romans 6:23 states that the cost of sin is death. Jesus came to absorb the consequences of our sins. Even though we deserve death, Jesus died in our place. Because of this, God pours His grace (not wrath or condemnation) on us. Jesus provided the way to become cleansed of our sins and sanctified before God (John 17:9-19, Hebrews 12-13). All He asks in return for this gift is described in Matthew 22:34-40 – love God and love our neighbors just as God demonstrated His love toward us. Also, the work of the law is written in our hearts (Romans 2:12-16).

God was angry when the Israelites constructed and worshiped a golden calf (Exodus 32:7-10). When Moses was away, the Israelites constructed an idol made of gold. Then they worshiped it. This broke God's fundamental commandment – You shall have no other gods before me (Exodus 20:3, Deuteronomy 5:7). Before Moses had a chance to respond, God condemned them to death. Moses pleaded with God to spare them. Moses spoke boldly to God reminding Him of the promises He made to the descendants of Abraham, Isaac, and Jacob. God was deeply moved and relented. In a parallel passage, Jesus was angry and drove the corrupt money changers out of the temple (John 2:13-17). They desecrated the temple and lost sight of what it meant to glorify and worship God. Even though we all deserve death, Jesus pleaded on our behalf and took those consequences upon Himself.

"My Presence shall go with you, and I will give you rest" (Exodus 33:14). "Come unto Me, all you that labor and are heavy laden, and I will give you rest (Matthew 11:28). These parallel passages clearly define a gift given by God to those who believe and follow – rest. Believers are promised a time in which we do not have to worry or perform heavy labor.

Offering of free will sacrifices (Leviticus 22:18-19). Be a living sacrifice (Romans 12:1). Jesus demonstrates what it is to be a living sacrifice and sacrificial love. We as believers are called to carry those burdens as we follow Him. Before the crucifixion and resurrection of Jesus Christ, believers were called to perform forms of sacrifice in a prescribed manner that glorifies God.

Israeli camp configuration in the wilderness forms a cross (Numbers 2). The camp layout in Numbers 1-2 of the tribes of Israel are very specific in its detail. The picture shown below is a visual representation of these instructions. The tribes of Dan, Naphtali, and Asher in the north totaled 157,600 and were under the banner of the Eagle. The tribes of Reuben, Simeon, and Gad in the south totaled 151,400 and were under the banner of a Man. The tribes of Ephraim, Manasseh, and Benjamin in the west totaled 108,100 and were under the banner of the Ox. The tribes of Judah, Issachar, and Zebulun in the east totaled 186,400 and were under the banner of the Lion. The tribe of Levi was not numbered and placed in the center, which symbolized the priestly nature and duties of Jesus when He died on the cross (Mark 15:21-41).

The standard, banner, or flag, displayed by every division composed of three tribes denotes an army united under one leader. Neither Mosaic law, nor the Old Testament, gives us any idea as to the form or character of these standards. According to rabbinical tradition, the standard of Judah was a lion, the standard of Reuben was the likeness of a man, the standard of Ephraim was an ox, and the standard of Dan was an eagle. These symbols in the layout described are mentioned in Ezekiel 1:10: "As for the likeness of their faces, they four had the face of a man, and the face of a lion, on the right side: and they four had the face of an ox on the left side; they four also had the face of an eagle [KJV]." There is a similar passage in Revelation 4:6-7, "Before the throne there was a sea of glass like unto crystal: and in the midst of the throne, and round about the throne, were four beasts full of eyes before and behind. And the first beast was like a lion, and the second beast like a calf, and the third beast had a face as a man, and the fourth beast was like a flying eagle [KJV]."

Promise Keeper

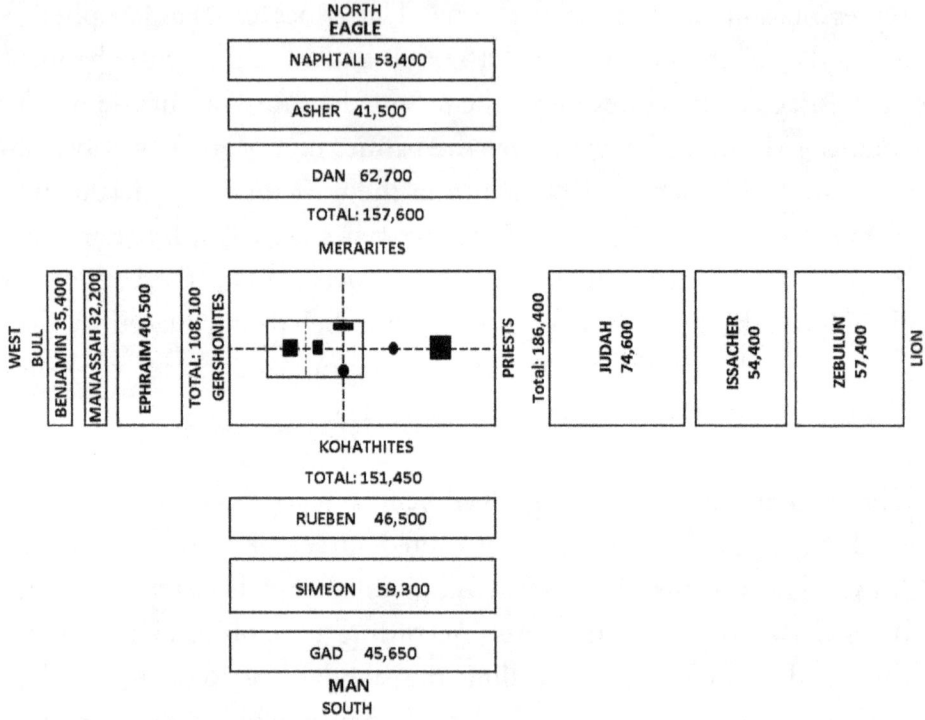

Two witnesses spoke to the nation of Israel about entering the Promised Land (Numbers 14:1-10). Joshua and Caleb encouraged Israel to enter the land promised to them by God. Similarly, two witnesses will speak to the world about entering heaven (Revelation 11:1-6). They are representatives of God and are given specific powers.

Moses intercedes for Israel (Numbers 14:11-25). Jesus intercedes for all believers (Hebrews 7:20-28).

"Go not up, for the Lord is not among you; that you be not smitten before your enemies [Numbers 14:42 - KJV]." "He that is faithful in that which is least is faithful also in much: and he that is unjust in the least is unjust also in much [Luke 16:10 - KJV]." Just as God gave the Israelites many opportunities to obey Him, He has given all of us many opportunities to turn away from sin and follow Him. Just as time ran out for Israel, it will also run out for us. God's mercy will only be poured out for so long. There will be a time of accountability for all of us.

Israel looked upon the Bronze Serpent for salvation (Numbers 21:4-9). Believers look to Jesus who died on the cross for our salvation (John 3:16). The Bronze Serpent is symbolic of the salvation provided by the crucifixion and resurrection of Jesus Christ.

Balaam struck the donkey three times then his eyes were opened (Numbers 22:22-40). Peter denied Jesus three times then he realized what happened (Luke 22:31-34, 54-62). In both instances, the faith of Balaam and Peter were weak. They were in denial of the truth that was right in front of them.

Israel is the chosen people (Deuteronomy 7:6-8). Jesus chose us before the foundation of the world (Ephesians 1:3-6). As part of being selected by God, these specifics groups are separated from the world and its values. Along with the separation comes a special promise or covenant. The Mosaic Covenant is related to bringing Israel out from bondage of Egypt and leading them to a land flowing with milk and honey. The New Covenant is the promise God has made between Him and the followers of Jesus Christ in that He will forgive sin and restore fellowship for all who believe in the power of the crucifixion and resurrection of the Messiah.

Chapter 9

Faith

"We are twice armed if we fight with faith."
- Plato

What is faith? To have faith is to invest your entire trust into someone or something. When we say to "have faith," it creates the incorrect idea that it is a state of being – that it is an object that we carry around with us.

Faith is more of an action than it is an object. Just as true love is a long-term consistency of selfless actions, faith is the consistent effort of investing trust into someone or something other than yourself.

We have taken you on a journey of discovery into the lives of Jesus and Moses. You have learned that words and numbers within the Bible have significant meaning. You have been introduced to the 7 Feasts of Israel as described in Leviticus 23. You have been given historical context of people, places and events within the Bible to gain a larger appreciation and understanding of them. We have shown you that both Jesus and Moses have demonstrated servant leadership.

Moses is a archetype or example of Jesus. There are numerous similarities and parallels between the two and we have explored them in detail. Most importantly, we have shown throughout this book that Jesus was there at the beginning of all things, that He sacrificed Himself for us with the full understanding of what that truly means, and that He will return as king and high priest. Faith in Jesus Christ as our redeemer and savior is a concept we should understand and continuously explore as believers. Romans 1:16-17 states, "For I am not ashamed of the gospel of Christ: for it is the power of God unto salvation to every one that believes; to the Jew first, and also to the Greek. For therein is the righteousness of God revealed from faith to faith: as it is written, 'The just shall live by faith' [KJV]."

To have faith in Jesus is to have faith in His promises. Faith is not a new concept. It has been around since at least the time of Abel – the son of Adam.

Hebrews 11: 4-40 [KJV]

v. 4-7) "By faith Abel offered unto God a more excellent sacrifice than Cain, by which he obtained witness that he was righteous, God testifying of his gifts: and by it he being dead yet speaks. By faith Enoch was translated that he should not see death; and was not found, because God had translated him: for before his translation he had this testimony, that he pleased God. But without faith it is impossible to please him: for he that comes to God must believe that He is, and that He is a rewarder of them that diligently seek Him. By faith Noah, being warned of God of things not seen as yet, moved with fear, prepared an ark to the saving of his house; by the which he condemned the world, and became heir of the righteousness which is by faith."

Cain and Abel wanted to worship God (Genesis 4:1-15). Both brought their offerings to God. Cain's sacrifice was not accepted (because he was selfish and prideful), whereas Abel's was (because he was humble and obedient). Enoch walked with God in faith (Genesis 5:21-24). Enoch pleased God and God took him up into heaven. God will reward the faithful. Noah received divine instruction from God (Genesis 6:9-9:29). As a faithful servant, Noah built a large boat far away from any major source of water and filled it with animals and his family.

v. 8-22) "By faith Abraham, when he was called to go out into a place which he should after receive for an inheritance, obeyed; and he went out, not knowing whither he went. By faith he sojourned in the land of promise, as in a strange country, dwelling in tabernacles with Isaac and Jacob, the heirs with him of the same promise: for he looked for a city which has foundations, whose builder and maker is God. Through faith also Sarah herself received strength to conceive seed, and was delivered of a child when she was past age, because she judged Him faithful who had promised. Therefore sprang there even of one, and him as good as dead, so many as the stars of the sky in multitude, and as the sand which is by the sea shore innumerable. These all died in faith, not having received the promises, but having seen them afar off, and were persuaded of them, and embraced them, and confessed that they were strangers and pilgrims on the earth. For they that say such things declare plainly that they seek a country. And truly, if they had been mindful of that country from where they came out, they might have had opportunity to have returned. But now they desire a better country, that is, an heavenly: wherefore God is not ashamed to be called their God: for He has prepared for them a city. By faith Abraham, when he was tried, offered up Isaac: and he that had received the promises offered up his only begotten son, of whom it was said, 'That in Isaac shall thy seed be called:' accounting that God was able to raise him up, even from the dead; from where also he received him in a figure. By faith Isaac blessed Jacob and Esau concerning things to come. By faith Jacob, when he was a dying, blessed both the sons of Joseph; and worshiped, leaning upon the top of his staff. By faith Joseph, when he died, made mention of the departing of the children of Israel; and gave commandment concerning his bones."

If you take a literal and conservative interpretation of the genealogy described in Genesis 11, Abraham's father – Terah – may have had the opportunity to talk to Noah directly. Likewise, Abraham may have had the opportunity to talk to Noah's son – Shem – directly. These first-hand experiences of the Great Flood may have been passed down to Abraham by those who lived through it. Abraham had a firm faith in God's promises (Genesis 12-25). He demonstrated his strong faith by nearly following through on God's command to sacrifice the son who was to be heir to his covenant with God. At the last moment, God provided a substitutionary sacrifice. Isaac followed God's command and stayed in the land of the Philistines. Because of his faith, God blessed Isaac with physical wealth (Genesis 25-28). By faith Jacob stayed in the Promised Land until God told him to move to Egypt, even though his family was in Egypt (Genesis 28-35). By faith Joseph went from being a slave to Egypt's second most powerful person in the empire (Genesis 37-50).

v. 23-31) "By faith Moses, when he was born, was hid three months of his parents, because they saw he was a proper child; and they were not afraid of the king's commandment. By faith Moses, when he was come to years, refused to be called the son of Pharaoh's daughter; choosing rather to suffer affliction with the people of God, than to enjoy the pleasures of sin for a season; esteeming the reproach of Christ greater riches than the treasures in Egypt: for he had respect unto the recompense of the reward. By faith he forsook Egypt, not fearing the wrath of the king: for he endured, as seeing him who is invisible. Through faith he kept the Passover, and the sprinkling of blood, lest he that destroyed the firstborn should touch them. By faith they passed through the Red Sea as by dry land: which the Egyptians assaying to do were drowned. By faith the walls of Jericho fell down, after they were compassed about seven days. By faith the harlot Rahab perished not with them that believed not, when she had received the spies with peace."

It is through faith that Moses led the Israelites out of Egypt. It is through faith that Joshua led the Israelites into the Promised Land and claimed it as their own. It is through faith that Rahab chose to help hide the spies from Israel, even though it meant almost certain death.

v. 32-40) "What shall I more say? For the time would fail me to tell of Gideon, and of Barak, and of Samson, and of Jephthah; of David also, and Samuel, and of the prophets: who through faith subdued kingdoms, wrought righteousness, obtained promises, stopped the mouths of lions. Quenched the violence of fire, escaped the edge of the sword, out of weakness were made strong, waxed valiant in fight, turned to flight the armies of the aliens. Women received their dead raised to life again: and others were tortured, not accepting deliverance; that they might obtain a better resurrection: and others had trial of cruel mockings and scourgings, yea, moreover of bonds and imprisonment: they were stoned, they were sawn asunder, were tempted, were slain with the sword: they wandered about in sheepskins and goatskins; being destitute, afflicted, tormented; they wandered in deserts, and in mountains, and in dens and caves of the earth. And these all, having obtained a good report through faith, received not the promise: God having provided some better thing for us, that they without us should not be made perfect."

Jesus had not yet been sacrificed on the cross for our sins, but those who lived prior to that event, believed in its promise. They demonstrated faith in God's promises and covenants. Abraham left all that he knew to become the genetic father of Jews, Arabs, and other Middle Eastern groups. It is through his faith that he became the spiritual father of both Jews and Christians. Moses followed in faith in such a way that he mimicked and demonstrated many of the events and principles related to Jesus' time of Earth.

It is by faith the repentant sinner is saved (Acts 16:31). It is by faith that Christ dwells in our hearts (Ephesians 3:17). It is by faith we are sanctified (Acts 26:18). It is by faith that we fight the good fight (1 Timothy 6:12). It is by faith the Devil is successfully resisted (1 Peter 5:9). It is by faith we have access to God (Ephesians 3:12).

What is the difference between faith and trust? Faith is a strong belief in someone or something without proof. Trust is a firm reliance on the character or integrity of another with proof. We as Christians are called to have faith in the redemptive works of Jesus Christ – that He died for us to restore us back into a relationship with God. We come to the cross as we are: broken, inexperienced, and full of ourselves. God heals that and begins a good work in us. As we learn and grow, our relationship with God shifts from one of faith to one of trust. Because of reading the Bible and our own personal relationship with God, we understand promises made by Him are promises kept. We begin to rely on His understanding, His strength, and His will. We understand through experience exactly what it means to be Christ-like. As we grow in faith, we are called to

Promise Keeper

trust in the Lord and rely on Him completely. God wants us to hold Him accountable to the promises He has made to us and wait for them to happen in His timing.

God wants to pour His grace upon us. Jesus wants to have a relationship with us. We have seen the promises described by Moses and others be fulfilled by the life and death of Christ Jesus. The next step is yours. It is up to you to hold God and Jesus accountable to those promises through your own faith and trust. God's will does prevail. Satan will be bound as promised in the Book of Revelation. Are you ready?

Epilogue

We have covered a lot of material in this book. Do not get bogged down in the muck and the mire. As stated repeatedly, the Bible has a simple message that is repeated over and over again in a number of different ways.

God so loved us that He who created the universe is willing to give up everything in order to have a relationship with you. The very first step is for you to receive this gift given freely that you could never repay.

The next steps are to pray, read the Bible (and books like this), and humbly serve the needs of others.

To be a Christian is to be Christ-like. Follow His lead.

May God bless you.

Promise Keeper

About the Authors

Michael Beaumont

"For those who follow Christ, and want to be more like Him, we have this hunger and thirst to learn more, to do more, and to become more, so that we can be an effective beacon of truth to the world."
- Michael Beaumont

I have been a Christian for as long as I can remember. I grew up in a Baptist church in Southern California. I have been involved in numerous Christian summer camps as both a participant and as an employee. The stories of Noah, Abraham, Joseph, Moses, Joshua, Samson, Jonah, Jesus, and Paul are etched permanently into my memory and my life. I directly battled alternative viewpoints as a college student studying Geology, Archaeology, Paleontology, and Evolutionary Biology. It took many years to work through these distinct concepts of reality. It would have been very easy to abandon my faith in God and replace it with a construct based on facts and the scientific method. After decades of study, I began to understand that science and Christianity are not and have never in conflict with each other. My walk with Christ became stronger by understanding three truths.

1) Science cannot answer every question.

Science cannot answer questions related to purpose or motive. It cannot answer questions that start with "Why." Science is limited to studying things we can hear, see, smell, taste, or touch.

2) Time had a beginning.

Even though modern science and the Christian faith have differences in how they interpret data, there is an undeniable truth in which both agree – time had a beginning. Think about how important a concept this is. If time always was and always will be, there was no beginning and we did not have to develop an explanation or cause. However, since time, the universe, and everything within it had a beginning, scientists are faced with the dilemma of trying to explain how everything started from nothing.

3) The Bible has never been wrong.

There are numerous details within the Bible that we can apply the scientific approach to. We obtain facts and interpret the data. The more information we gather, the more obvious it becomes that the information in the Bible is correct. I have studied many apparent inconsistencies within the Bible. It becomes obvious that after some study either our assumptions are incorrect or our interpretation of the facts are incorrect. So if the Bible has never been proven wrong, then we must learn why it is right. This was just the beginning of my journey as a follower of Christ.

I have several educational degrees, including a Bachelor in Geology, minor in Zoology, Secondary Education Teaching Credential in the field of Science, and a Master in Information Technology. I have learned numerous human and technology-related languages, been self-employed in the fields of Marketing and Business Development for over ten years, and have been associated with 6 published books on leadership, mentoring, business development, history, and Biblical truth.

If there is anything other people should truly understand is that life is not complicated. It may be difficult, but it is not complex. Most of us know that smoking and excessive drinking are unhealthy, but we choose not to give them up. Most of us know that a poor diet and lack of exercise are the primary causes of obesity, but we try to find alternative methods to fix the problem. Likewise, the path to eternal life with God is not complicated – believe in Jesus as our Savior – but we choose not to accept it. Keep life simple. Seek God first. Seek God always. He will tend to your wants and needs.

Reverend Emmarex Okhakhu, PhD

Emmarex Okhakhu was involved in reviewing the content of this book. His educational background includes Healthcare Administration, Theology, Counseling, Project Management, Clinical Research, and Organizational Management. He has spent much of his adult life within the healthcare industry providing a variety of services, including: chaplain, business development, compliance, chief operating officer, risk management, and leadership.

Bibliography

Chapter 1: Why This Book Is Important

"Best Selling Book of Non-Fiction." Gusiness Book of World Records. http://www.guinnessworldrecords.com/world-records/best-selling-book-of-non-fiction. July 15, 2017.

"Biblical Translation." Britannica. https://www.britannica.com/topic/biblical-translation. July 15, 2017.

"List of Religious Populations." Wikipedia. https://en.wikipedia.org/wiki/List_of_religious_populations. July 15, 2017.

"15 Flood Myths Similar to the Story of Noah." Comparative Religious Studies. http://blog.mythoreligio.com/15-flood-myths-similar-to-the-story-of-noah-2/. July 15, 2017.

"Books of the Bible." Blue Letter Bible. https://www.blueletterbible.org/study/misc/66books.cfm. July 15, 2017.

"List of Christian Denominations." Wikipedia. https://en.wikipedia.org/wiki/List_of_Christian_denominations. July 15, 2017.

"Masoretic Text." Wikipedia. https://en.wikipedia.org/wiki/Masoretic_Text. July 15, 2017.

"Septuagint." Wikipedia. https://en.wikipedia.org/wiki/Septuagint. July 15, 2017.

"Athanasius of Alexandria." Wikipedia. https://en.wikipedia.org/wiki/Athanasius_of_Alexandria. July 15, 2017.

"Biblical Apocrypha." Wikipedia. https://en.wikipedia.org/wiki/Biblical_apocrypha. July 15, 2017.

Jones, Dr Stephen. "Chronology of the Septuagint Text." God's Kingdom Ministries. http://www.gods-kingdom-ministries.net/daily-weblogs/2008/08-2008/chronology-of-the-septuagint-text/. July 15, 2017.

"Hanukkah." Wikipedia. https://en.wikipedia.org/wiki/Hanukkah. July 15, 2017.

"King James Version." Wikipedia. https://en.wikipedia.org/wiki/King_James_Version. July 15, 2017.

"New King James Version NKJV Bible ." Bible Gateway. https://www.biblegateway.com/versions/New-King-James-Version-NKJV-Bible/. July 15, 2017.

Chapter 2: Languages of the Bible

"Language." Wikipedia. https://en.wikipedia.org/wiki/Language. July 15, 2017.

"Iliad." Wikipedia. https://en.wikipedia.org/wiki/Iliad. July 15, 2017.

"The Art of War." Wikipedia. https://en.wikipedia.org/wiki/The_Art_of_War. July 15, 2017.

"Meditations." Wikipedia. https://en.wikipedia.org/wiki/Meditations. July 15, 2017.

"History of Writing." Wikipedia. https://en.wikipedia.org/wiki/History_of_writing. July 15, 2017.

"Egyptian Hieroglyphs." Wikipedia. https://en.wikipedia.org/wiki/Egyptian_hieroglyphs. July 15, 2017.

"Rosetta Stone." Wikipedia. https://en.wikipedia.org/wiki/Rosetta_Stone. July 15, 2017.

"Jean François Champollion." Wikipedia. https://en.wikipedia.org/wiki/Jean-Fran%C3%A7ois_Champollion. July 15, 2017.

"Right to Left." Wikipedia. https://en.wikipedia.org/wiki/Right-to-left. July 15, 2017.

"Phoenicia." Wikipedia. https://en.wikipedia.org/wiki/Phoenicia. July 15, 2017.

"Semitic Languages." Wikipedia. https://en.wikipedia.org/wiki/Semitic_languages. July 15, 2017.

Schwab, Marianne. "Jerusalem: The Eye of the Needle Gate." Best Travel Deals Tips. http://www.best-travel-deals-tips.com/jerusalem-eye-of-the-needle-gate.html. July 15, 2017.

"On the Difference Between Greek Thought and Hebrew Thought." Edge Induced Cohesion. https://edgeinducedcohesion.wordpress.com/2010/12/22/on-the-difference-between-greek-thought-and-hebrew-thought/. July 15, 2017.

Missler, Chuck. "A Hidden Message: The Gospel in Genesis." Koinonia House. http://www.khouse.org/articles/1996/44/. July 15, 2017.

"Why Are There Four Gospels." Blue Letter Bible. http://blogs.blueletterbible.org/blb/2012/12/11/why-are-there-four-gospels/. July 15, 2017.

"Paul the Apostle." Wikipedia. https://en.wikipedia.org/wiki/Paul_the_Apostle. July 15, 2017.

"Greek Words For Love." McLean Bible Church. https://www.mcleanbible.org/sites/default/files/Multiply-Resources/Chap3/GreekWordsforLoveWS_Chapter3.pdf. July 15, 2017.

"The Four Loves." Wikipedia. https://en.wikipedia.org/wiki/The_Four_Loves. July 15, 2017.

Sproul, R.C. "Ancient Promises." Ligonier Ministries. http://www.ligonier.org/learn/articles/ancient-promises/. July 15, 2017.

"Augustine of Hippo." Wikipedia. https://en.wikipedia.org/wiki/Augustine_of_Hippo. July 15, 2017.

"The Jewish Holidays." Hebrew 4 Christians. http://www.hebrew4christians.com/Holidays/Introduction/introduction.html. July 15, 2017.

Chapter 3: Numbers in the Bible

"Stephen Langton." Wikipedia. https://en.wikipedia.org/wiki/Stephen_Langton. July 15, 2017.

"Magna Carta." Wikipedia. https://en.wikipedia.org/wiki/Magna_Carta. July 15, 2017.

Chapter 4: Seven Feasts

Rich, Tracey. "Jewish Calendar." Judaism 101. http://www.jewfaq.org/calendar.htm. July 15, 2017.

"Passover." Hebrew 4 Christians. http://www.hebrew4christians.com/Holidays/Spring_Holidays/Pesach/pesach.html. July 15, 2017.

"Unleavened Bread." Hebrew 4 Christians. http://www.hebrew4christians.com/Holidays/Spring_Holidays/Unleavened_Bread/Anavah/anavah.html. July 15, 2017.

"First Fruits." Hebrew 4 Christians. http://www.hebrew4christians.com/Holidays/Spring_Holidays/First_Fruits/first_fruits.html. July 15, 2017.

Gordon, I. "Genesis 8." Jesus Plus Nothing. http://www.jesusplusnothing.com/studies/quick/genesis8.htm. July 15, 2017.

"Events on Nisan 17" Five Doves. http://www.fivedoves.com/letters/feb2014/dp221-1.htm. July 15, 2017.

"Shavuot." Wikipedia. https://en.wikipedia.org/wiki/Shavuot. July 15, 2017.

"Shavuot." Jews for Jesus. https://jewsforjesus.org/publications/newsletter/june-2005/shavuot. July 15, 2017.

Lane, Mark. "Feast of Pentecost." Bible Numbers for Life. https://biblenumbers.files.wordpress.com/2012/08/feast-of-pentecost.pdf. July 15, 2017.

"Book of Judges: Samson and Delilah." The Sacred Calendar. http://www.thesacredcalendar.com/book-of-judges-samson-and-delilah/. July 15, 2017.

"How Many Times Is Passover Mentioned in the Bible." Answers. http://www.answers.com/Q/How_many_times_is_Passover_mentioned_in_the_bible?#slide=2. July 15, 2017.

"Feast of Weeks." Bible Gateway. https://www.biblegateway.com/quicksearch/?quicksearch=feast+of+weeks&qs_version=NKJV. July 15, 2017.

"Wheat Harvest." Bible Gateway. https://www.biblegateway.com/quicksearch/?quicksearch=wheat+harvest&qs_version=NKJV. July 15, 2017.

Guzik, David. "Judges 15 Commentary." Enduring Word. https://enduringword.com/commentary/judges-15/. July 15, 2017.

Rea, Hazel; Gladwell, Chris. "Ruth Obeys God and Finds Love." Easy English. http://www.easyenglish.info/bible-commentary/ruth-lbw.htm. July 15, 2017.

Guzik, David. "1 Samuel 6 Commentary." Enduring Word. https://enduringword.com/commentary/1-samuel-6/. July 15, 2017.

"Rosh Hashanah." Wikipedia. https://en.wikipedia.org/wiki/Rosh_Hashanah. July 15, 2017.

"Rosh Hashannah." Hebrew 4 Christians. http://www.hebrew4christians.com/Holidays/Fall_Holidays/Rosh_Hashannah/rosh_hashannah.html. July 15, 2017.

"Jesus' Birth Day." Feasts of the Lord. http://www.feastsofthelord.net/id136.html. July 15, 2017.

"The Birth of Jesus and the Feast of Trumpets." Associates for Scriptural Knowledge. http://www.askelm.com/star/star008.htm. July 15, 2017.

Zeolla, Gary. "Jesus Born in September." Darkness to Light. http://www.dtl.org/jesus/christmas/born-september.htm. July 15, 2017.

"Yom Kippur." Hebrew 4 Christians. http://www.hebrew4christians.com/Holidays/Fall_Holidays/Yom_Kippur/yom_kippur.html. July 15, 2017.

"Sukkot." Hebrew 4 Christians. http://www.hebrew4christians.com/Holidays/Fall_Holidays/Sukkot/sukkot.html. July 15, 2017.

Chapter 5: Bible as History

"Cicero." Wikipedia. https://en.wikipedia.org/wiki/Cicero. July 15, 2017.

"Siege of Jerusalem (63 BC)." Wikipedia. https://en.wikipedia.org/wiki/Siege_of_Jerusalem_(63_BC). July 15, 2017.

"Assassination of Julius Caesar." Wikipedia. https://en.wikipedia.org/wiki/Assassination_of_Julius_Caesar. July 15, 2017.

"What Is History." History Guide. http://www.historyguide.org/history.html. July 15, 2017.

"Geocentric Model." Wikipedia. https://en.wikipedia.org/wiki/Geocentric_model. July 15, 2017.

"Ptolemy." Wikipedia. https://en.wikipedia.org/wiki/Ptolemy. July 15, 2017.

"Nicolaus_Copernicus." Wikipedia. https://en.wikipedia.org/wiki/Nicolaus_Copernicus. July 15, 2017.

"Johannes_Kepler." Wikipedia. https://en.wikipedia.org/wiki/Johannes_Kepler. July 15, 2017.

"Galileo_Galilei." Wikipedia. https://en.wikipedia.org/wiki/Galileo_Galilei. July 15, 2017.

"Heliocentrism." Wikipedia. https://en.wikipedia.org/wiki/Heliocentrism. July 15, 2017.

"Isaac_Newton." Wikipedia. https://en.wikipedia.org/wiki/Isaac_Newton. July 15, 2017.

Wansley, W.R. "The Heavens Mark the Passing of Sir Isaac Newton." American Thinker. http://www.americanthinker.com/blog/2015/03/the_heavens_mark_the_passing_of_sir_isaac_newton.html. July 15, 2017.

"Land of Goshen." Wikipedia. https://en.wikipedia.org/wiki/Land_of_Goshen. July 15, 2017.

"Qantir." Wikipedia. https://en.wikipedia.org/wiki/Qantir. July 15, 2017.

"Vizier (Ancient Egypt)." Wikipedia. https://en.wikipedia.org/wiki/Vizier_(Ancient_Egypt). July 15, 2017.

"Route of the Hebrews from Egypt to Mt Sinai." True Discoveries. http://truediscoveries.org/wp-content/uploads/RS2.jpg. July 15, 2017.

"Gulf_of_Suez." Wikipedia. https://en.wikipedia.org/wiki/Gulf_of_Suez. July 15, 2017.

"Solomon." Wikipedia. https://en.wikipedia.org/wiki/Solomon. July 15, 2017.

"Pontius Pilate." Wikipedia. https://en.wikipedia.org/wiki/Pontius_Pilate. July 15, 2017.

"Ur Kaśdim." Wikipedia. https://en.wikipedia.org/wiki/Ur_Ka%C5%9Bdim. July 15, 2017.

"Mesopotamia." Wikipedia. https://en.wikipedia.org/wiki/Mesopotamia. July 15, 2017.

"Sargon of Akkad." Wikipedia. https://en.wikipedia.org/wiki/Sargon_of_Akkad. July 15, 2017.

"Akkadian_Empire." Wikipedia. https://en.wikipedia.org/wiki/Akkadian_Empire. July 15, 2017.

"Shar-Kali-Sharri." Wikipedia. https://en.wikipedia.org/wiki/Shar-Kali-Sharri. July 15, 2017.

"Gutian People." Wikipedia. https://en.wikipedia.org/wiki/Gutian_people. July 15, 2017.

"Sumer." Wikipedia. https://en.wikipedia.org/wiki/Sumer. July 15, 2017.

"Sumerian King List." Wikipedia. https://en.wikipedia.org/wiki/Sumerian_King_List. July 15, 2017.

"Third Dynasty of Ur." Wikipedia. https://en.wikipedia.org/wiki/Third_Dynasty_of_Ur. July 15, 2017.

"Elam." Wikipedia. https://en.wikipedia.org/wiki/Elam. July 15, 2017.

"Tunguska Event." Wikipedia. https://en.wikipedia.org/wiki/Tunguska_event. July 15, 2017.

"Meteorite." Wikipedia. https://en.wikipedia.org/wiki/Meteorite. July 15, 2017.

"Amenemhat III." Wikipedia. https://en.wikipedia.org/wiki/Amenemhat_III. July 15, 2017.

"Senusret III." Wikipedia. https://en.wikipedia.org/wiki/Senusret_III. July 15, 2017.

"Faiyum Oasis." Wikipedia. https://en.wikipedia.org/wiki/Faiyum_Oasis. July 15, 2017.

Breasted, James. "Ancient Records of Egypt, Volume 1." Giza Pyramids. http://www.gizapyramids.org/pdf_library/breasted_ancient_records_ I.pdf. July 15, 2017.

"Merneferre Ay." Wikipedia. https://en.wikipedia.org/wiki/Merneferre_Ay. July 15, 2017.

"Hyksos." Wikipedia. https://en.wikipedia.org/wiki/Hyksos. July 15, 2017.

"List of Pharaohs." Wikipedia. https://en.wikipedia.org/wiki/List_of_pharaohs. July 15, 2017.

"John Garstang." Wikipedia. https://en.wikipedia.org/wiki/John_Garstang. July 15, 2017.

"Kathleen Kenyon." Wikipedia. https://en.wikipedia.org/wiki/Kathleen_Kenyon. July 15, 2017.

Ashley, Scott; Aust, Jerold. "Jericho: Does the Evidence Disprove or Prove the Bible." Associates For Biblical Research. http://www.biblearchaeology.org/post/2009/01/Jericho-Does-the-Evidence-Disprove-or-Prove-the-Bible.aspx. July 15, 2017.

"Bryant G. Wood." Wikipedia. https://en.wikipedia.org/wiki/Bryant_G._Wood. July 15, 2017.

"Augustus." Wikipedia. https://en.wikipedia.org/wiki/Augustus. July 15, 2017.

"Quirinius." Wikipedia. https://en.wikipedia.org/wiki/Quirinius. July 15, 2017.

"Herod_the_Great." Wikipedia. https://en.wikipedia.org/wiki/Herod_the_Great. July 15, 2017.

"Tiberius." Wikipedia. https://en.wikipedia.org/wiki/Tiberius. July 15, 2017.

"Jubilee (Biblical)." Wikipedia. https://en.wikipedia.org/wiki/Jubilee_(biblical). July 15, 2017.

"Josephus." Wikipedia. https://en.wikipedia.org/wiki/Josephus. July 15, 2017.

"Antiquities of the Jews - Book XVII." Sacred Texts. http://www.sacred-texts.com/jud/josephus/ant-17.htm. July 15, 2017.

"Herod's Death, Jesus' Birth and a Lunar Eclipse." Biblical Archaeology Society. http://www.biblicalarchaeology.org/daily/people-cultures-in-the-bible/jesus-historical-jesus/herods-death-jesus-birth-and-a-lunar-eclipse/. July 15, 2017.

Ramsay, William. "Quirinius the Governor of Syria." Bible Hub. http://biblehub.com/library/ramsay/was_christ_born_in_bethlehem/chapter_11_quirinius_the_governor.htm. July 15, 2017.

"Herod Antipas." Wikipedia. https://en.wikipedia.org/wiki/Herod_Antipas. July 15, 2017.

"Philip the Tetrarch." Wikipedia. https://en.wikipedia.org/wiki/Philip_the_Tetrarch. July 15, 2017.

"Caiaphas." Wikipedia. https://en.wikipedia.org/wiki/Caiaphas. July 15, 2017.

"Passover Dates 26-34 AD." Judaism Is My Christianity. http://www.judaismvschristianity.com/passover_dates.htm. July 15, 2017.

Missler, Chuck. "Israel's New Year Begins: The Feast of Trumpets." Koinonia House. http://www.khouse.org/articles/1995/105/. July 15, 2017.

Smith, Gary. "Ezra, Nehemiah, Esther." Cornerstone Biblical Commentary. https://books.google.com/books?id=Rv_RCwAAQBAJ&pg=PA66. July 15, 2017.

"Second Temple." Conservapedia. http://www.conservapedia.com/Second_Temple. July 15, 2017.

"Jesus' Triumphal Entry On Palm Sunday - The Day He Was Presented to Israel As Their Messiah-King." Cutting Edge Ministries. http://www.cuttingedge.org/news/n2278.cfm. July 15, 2017.

"Septuagint." Wikipedia. https://en.wikipedia.org/wiki/Septuagint. July 15, 2017.

Hasel, Gerhard PhD. "New Light on the Book of Daniel from the Dead Sea Scrolls." Associates For Biblical Research. http://www.biblearchaeology.org/post/2012/07/31/New-Light-on-the-Book-of-Daniel-from-the-Dead-Sea-Scrolls.aspx#Article. July 15, 2017.

Richard, Ed. "Prophecies of the Destruction of Jerusalem in A.D. 70 - Lesson 2: The Holocaust in Daniel 9." The Moorings. http://www.themoorings.org/Bible_prophecy/holocaust_in_AD_70/Daniel_9.html. July 15, 2017.

Belibtreu, Erika. "Grisly Assyrian Record of Torture and Death." University of Massachusetts Lowell. http://faculty.uml.edu/ethan_Spanier/Teaching/documents/CP6.0AssyrianTorture.pdf. July 15, 2017.

"A Staggering Archaelogical Discovery - The Mighty Assyrian Empire Emerges From the Dust." United Church of God. https://www.ucg.org/bible-study-tools/booklets/is-the-bible-true/a-staggering-archaelogical-discovery-the-mighty. July 15, 2017.

"Kingdom of Israel (Samaria)." Wikipedia. https://en.wikipedia.org/wiki/Kingdom_of_Israel_(Samaria). July 15, 2017.

"Neo-Assyrian Empire." Wikipedia. https://en.wikipedia.org/wiki/Neo-Assyrian_Empire. July 15, 2017.

"Neo-Babylonian Empire." Wikipedia. https://en.wikipedia.org/wiki/Neo-Babylonian_Empire. July 15, 2017.

"Nebuchadnezzar II." Wikipedia.
https://en.wikipedia.org/wiki/Nebuchadnezzar_II. July 15, 2017.

Wood, Bryant PhD. "Israelite Kings in Assyrian Inscriptions." Associates For Biblical Research. http://www.biblearchaeology.org/post/2012/05/22/Israelite-Kings-in-Assyrian-Inscriptions.aspx#Article. July 15, 2017.

"The Babylonian Chronicles." Bible History Online. http://www.bible-history.com/archaeology/babylon/babylonian-chronicle.html. July 15, 2017.

"Ramesses II." Wikipedia. https://en.wikipedia.org/wiki/Ramesses_II. July 15, 2017.

"Merneptah Stele." Wikipedia. https://en.wikipedia.org/wiki/Merneptah_Stele. July 15, 2017.

"Merneptah." Wikipedia. https://en.wikipedia.org/wiki/Merneptah. July 15, 2017.

"Amarna Letters." Wikipedia. https://en.wikipedia.org/wiki/Amarna_letters. July 15, 2017.

"Habiru." Wikipedia. https://en.wikipedia.org/wiki/Habiru. July 15, 2017.

Rudd, Steve. "Solution to the Chronology of the Book of Judges." Wikipedia. http://www.bible.ca/archeology/bible-archeology-exodus-route-date-chronology-of-judges.htm. July 15, 2017.

"Aram-Naharaim." Wikipedia. https://en.wikipedia.org/wiki/Aram-Naharaim. July 15, 2017.

"Mitanni." Wikipedia. https://en.wikipedia.org/wiki/Mitanni. July 15, 2017.

"Late Bronze Age Collapse." Wikipedia. https://en.wikipedia.org/wiki/Late_Bronze_Age_collapse. July 15, 2017.

"Medinet Habu (Temple)." Wikipedia. https://en.wikipedia.org/wiki/Medinet_Habu_(temple). July 15, 2017.

"Ramesses III." Wikipedia. https://en.wikipedia.org/wiki/Ramesses_III. July 15, 2017.

"Sea Peoples." Wikipedia. https://en.wikipedia.org/wiki/Sea_Peoples. July 15, 2017.

"Tell_El-Dab'a." Wikipedia. https://en.wikipedia.org/wiki/Tell_El-Dab'a. July 15, 2017.

"Avaris." Wikipedia. https://en.wikipedia.org/wiki/Avaris. July 15, 2017.

Mahoney, Timothy. "Patterns of Evidence." Patterns of Evidence. http://patternsofevidence.com/. July 15, 2017.

"David Rohl." Wikipedia. https://en.wikipedia.org/wiki/David_Rohl. July 15, 2017.

"Taurids." Wikipedia. https://en.wikipedia.org/wiki/Taurids. July 15, 2017.

"Kaali Crater." Wikipedia. https://en.wikipedia.org/wiki/Kaali_crater. July 15, 2017.

"Campo del Cielo." Wikipedia. https://en.wikipedia.org/wiki/Campo_del_Cielo. July 15, 2017.

"Henbury Meteorites Conservation Reserve." Wikipedia. https://en.wikipedia.org/wiki/Henbury_Meteorites_Conservation_Reserve. July 15, 2017.

King, A. Roy. "Oxford Scholar: Egyptian History Is 'a Collection of Rags and Tatters'." A Roy King. https://aroyking.wordpress.com/2015/05/29/oxford-scholar-egyptian-history-is-a-collection-of-rags-and-tatters/. July 15, 2017.

Chapter 6: Trials and Tribulations

"Trumpet and Bowl Judgments: The End-Time Exodus Drama." People Get Ready. http://peoplegetready.org/end-times/seals-trumpets-bowls-series/trumpet-bowl-judgments-endtime-exodus-drama/. July 15, 2017.

Chapter 8: Parallels

"Numbers Chapter 2 Commentary." Sacred Texts. http://www.sacred-texts.com/bib/cmt/kad/num002.htm. July 15, 2017.

Appendix

"Solved: Divided Kingdom Period Chronology." Bible.ca. http://www.bible.ca/archeology/bible-archeology-maps-timeline-chronology-kings-prophets-assyrians-babylonians-egyptians-tisri-nisan-inclusive-accession-reckoning-divided-kingdom-dates-931-587bc.htm. July 15, 2017.

Appendix

Books of the Bible

Old Testament

Genesis
Exodus
Leviticus
Numbers
Deuteronomy
Joshua
Judges
Ruth
1 Samuel
2 Samuel
1 Kings
2 Kings
1 Chronicles
2 Chronicles
Ezra
Nehemiah
Esther
Job
Psalms
Proverbs
Ecclesiastes
Song of Solomon
Isaiah

New Testament

Matthew
Mark
Luke
John
Acts
Romans
1 Corinthians
2 Corinthians
Galatians
Ephesians
Philippians
Colossians
1 Thessalonians
2 Thessalonians
1 Timothy
2 Timothy
Titus
Philemon
Hebrews
James
1 Peter
2 Peter
1 John

Jeremiah
Lamentations
Ezekiel
Daniel
Hosea
Joel
Amos
Obadiah
Jonah
Micah
Nahum
Habakkuk
Zephaniah
Haggai
Zechariah
Malachi

2 John
3 John
Jude
Revelation

Apocrypha

1 Esdras
2 Esdras
1 Maccabees
2 Maccabees
Additions to Daniel
Additions to Esther
Book of Baruch
Book of Judith
Book of Wisdom
Epistle of Jeremiah
Prayer of Manasseh

Sirach
Tobit

Kings of United Israel: 1052-931 BC

King Saul (1052-1010 BC)
King David (1010-970 BC)
King Solomon (970-931 BC)

Kings of Israel: 931-723 BC

Jeroboam I (931-910 BC)
– 1 Kings 12:25-14:20
Nadab (910-909 BC)
– 1 Kings 15:25-31
Baasha (909-886 BC)
– 1 Kings 15:32-16:7
Elah (886-885 BC)
– 1 Kings 16:8-14
Zimri (885 BC)
– 1 Kings 16:15-20
Tibni (885-880 BC)
– 1 Kings 16:21-22
Omri (885-874 BC)
– 1 Ki 16:23-28
Ahab (874-853 BC)
– 1 Kings 16:28-34; 20:1-22:40
Ahaziah (853-852 BC)
– 1 Kings 22:40-53; 2 Kings 1:2-18
Joram (852-841 BC)
– 2 Kings 3

Jehu (841-814 BC)
– 2 Kings 9:11-10:36
Jehoahaz (814-798 BC)
– 2 Kings 13:1-9
Jehoash / Joash (793-782 BC)
– 2 Kings 13:10-25; 14:15-16
Jeroboam II (793-753 BC)
– 2 Kings 14:23-29
Zechariah (753-752 BC)
– 2 Kings 15:8-12
Shallum (752 BC)
– 2 Kings 15:13-15
Pekah (752-732 BC)
– 2 Ki 15:27-31
Menahem (752-742 BC)
– 2 Kings 15:16-22
Pekahiah (742-740 BC)
– 2 Ki 15:23-26
Hoshea (732-723 BC)
– 2 Kings 17:1-6

Kings of Judah: 931-587 BC

Rehoboam (931-914 BC)
– 1 Kings 14:21-31; 2 Chronicles 10-12
Abijah (914-911 BC)
– 1 Kings 15:1-8; 2 Chronicles 13:1-22
Asa (911-870 BC)
– 1 Kings 15:9-24; 2 Chronicles 14-16
Jehoshaphat (872-848 BC)
– 1 Kings 22:41-50; 2 Chronicles 17-20

Joram / Jehoram (853-841 BC)
- 2 Kings 8:16-24; 2 Chronicles 21
Ahaziah (841 BC)
- 2 Kings 8:25-29; 9:27-29; 2 Chronicles 22:1-9
Athaliah (841-835 BC)
- 2 Kings 11:1-16; 2 Chronicles 22:10-23:15
Joash / Jehoash (835-796 BC)
- 2 Kings 12; 2 Chronicles 23:16-24:27
Amaziah (796-767 BC)
- 2 Kings 14:1-20; 2 Chronicles 25
Uzziah / Azariah (790-739 BC)
- 2 Kings 14:21-22; 15:1-7; 2 Chronicles 26
Jotham (750-735 BC)
- 2 Kings 15:32-38; 2 Chronicles 27
Ahaz (735-715 BC)
- 2 Kings 16; 2 Chronicles 28
Hezekiah (786-728 BC)
- 2 Kings 18-20; 2 Chronicles 29-32
Manasseh (696-642 BC)
- 2 Kings 21:1-18; 2 Chronicles 33:1-20
Amon (642-640 BC)
- 2 Kings 21:19-26; 2 Chronicles 33:21-25
Josiah (640-609 BC)
- 2 Kings 22:1-23:30; 2 Chronicles 34-35
Jehoahaz (609 BC)
- 2 Kings 23:31-33
Jehoiakim (609-598 BC)
- 2 Kings 23:34-24:7
Jehoiachin (598-597 BC)
- 2 Kings 24:8-16

Promise Keeper

Zedekiah (597-587 BC)
– 2 Kings 24:18-25:26

Neo-Assyrian Empire Kings

Adad-nirari II (911-891 BC)
Tukulti-Ninurta II (891-884 BC)
Ashurnasirpal II (884-859 BC)
Shalmaneser III (859-824 BC)
Shamshi-Adad V (824-811 BC)
Adad-nirari III (811-783 BC
Shalmaneser IV (783-773 BC)
Ashur-dan III (772-755 BC)
Ashur-nirari V (755-745 BC)
Tiglath-Pileser III (745-727 BC)
Shalmaneser V (727-722 BC)
Sargon II (722-705 BC)
Sennacherib (705-681 BC)
Esarhaddon (681-669 BC)
Ashurbanipal (668-631 BC)
Ashur-etil-ilani (631-627 BC)
Sin-shumu-lishir (626 BC)
Sinsharishkun (626-612 BC)

Neo-Babylonian Empire Kings

Nabopolassar (626-605 BC)
Nebuchadnezzar II (605-562 BC)
Amel-Marduk / Merodach (562-560 BC)
Neriglissar / Nergal-Sharezer (560-556 BC)

Labashi-Marduk (556 BC)
Nabonidus (556-550 BC)
Belshazzar (550-539 BC)

www.ingramcontent.com/pod-product-compliance
Lightning Source LLC
Chambersburg PA
CBHW031143160426
43193CB00008B/234